THIS BOOK IS AIMED AT THOSE PEOPLE WHO WANT TO EXPRESS THEIR CREATIVE IDEAS AND TRANSFORM THEM INTO VISUAL REALITY IN THE SIMPLEST WAY POSSIBLE. WHETHER YOU'RE INTERESTED IN DIGITAL ART, PHOTOGRAPHY, GRAPHIC DESIGN, OR SIMPLY EXPANDING YOUR CREATIVE HORIZONS, THIS BOOK WILL PROVIDE YOU WITH THE TOOLS AND INSPIRATION YOU NEED TO GET STARTED. GET READY TO EXPLORE NEW FRONTIERS IN CREATIVITY AND DISCOVER THE EXCITING WORLD OF ARTIFICIAL INTELLIGENCE (AI) APPLIED TO IMAGING!

ALL PLATFORMS SHOWN IN THIS BOOK REQUIRE YOU TO REGISTER THROUGH A GOOGLE ACCOUNT. (EMAIL)

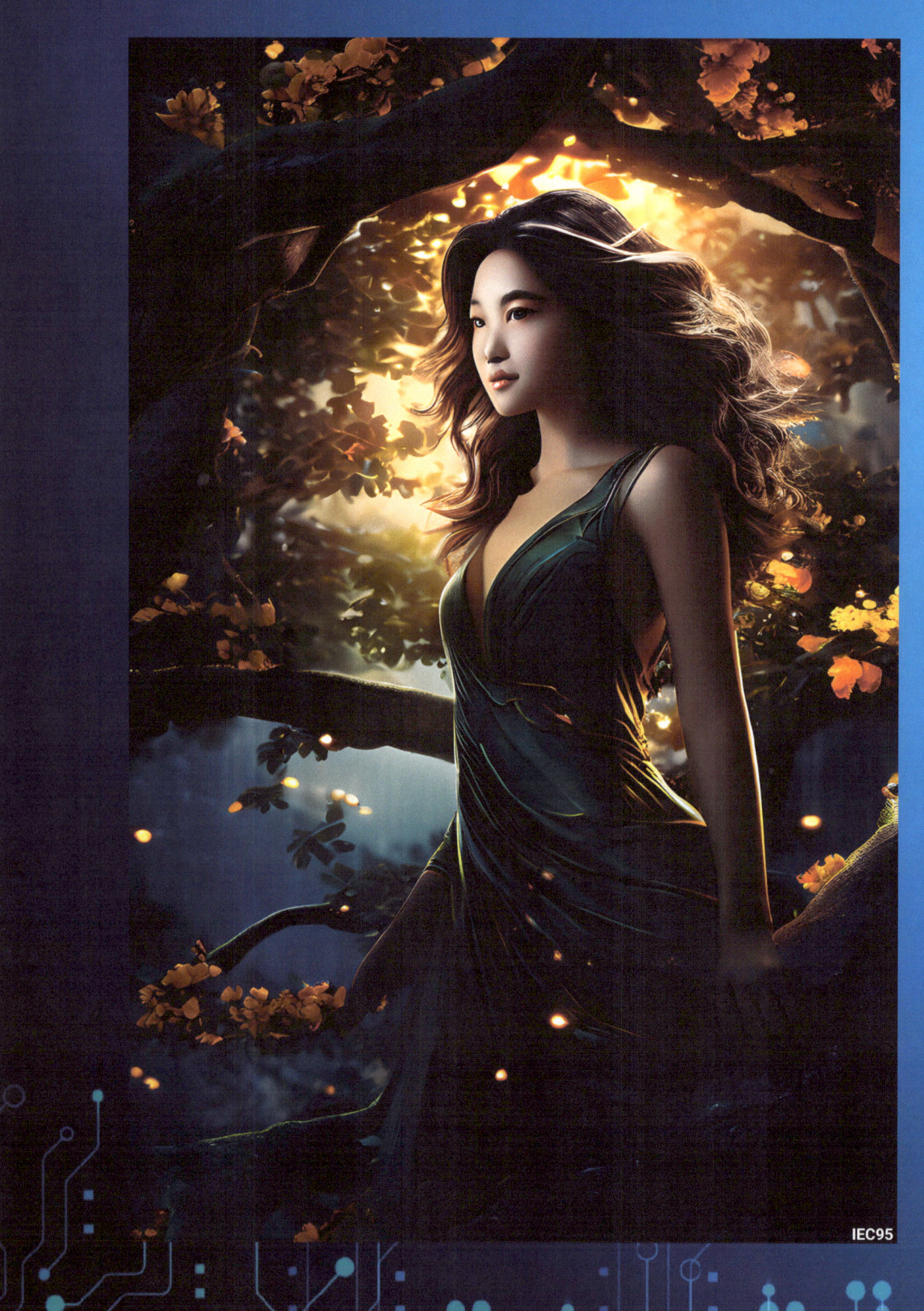

IEC95

BEFORE STARTING WE WANT TO SHOW YOU SOME BASIC TOOLS THAT YOU WILL FIND THROUGHOUT THE BOOK AND THAT KNOWING THE PURPOSE OF THESE WILL MAKE THE GUIDE EVEN EASIER.

PROMPT: THE PROMPT IS THE SPACE IN WHICH YOU WILL HAVE TO DESCRIBE THE IMAGE YOU WANT TO CREATE (THE MORE SPECIFIC AND DETAILED THE REQUEST, THE BETTER THE RESULT WILL BE)

NEGATIVE PROMPT: IN THIS SPACE YOU WILL HAVE TO DESCRIBE CHARACTERISTICS OR SPECIFIC INFORMATION THAT YOU WANT THE AI TO AVOID WHEN GENERATING THE IMAGE
EXAMPLE: DEFORMED, EXTRA LIMBS, NOISY, OUT OF FOCUS, BLURRY, ETC.

UPLOAD IMAGE: WITH THIS TOOL YOU CAN UPLOAD AN IMAGE OR PHOTO TO USE AS A REFERENCE AND CREATE YOUR OWN VERSION OF THAT IMAGE WITH DIFFERENT ANIMATION STYLES (IT IS ALSO RECOMMENDED TO DESCRIBE THE IMAGE IN THE PROMPT TO HELP THE AI BETTER UNDERSTAND THE CONTENT OF THE THE PICTURE)

IMAGE STRENGTH: THIS TOOL IS ACTIVATED WHEN UPLOADING AN IMAGE AND BY RAISING OR LOWERING THE STRENGTH WE WILL BE TELLING THE AI TO BE MORE OR LESS FAITHFUL TO THE REFERENCE IMAGE IN THE FINAL RESULT.

STYLE/FILTER/MODEL: ITS NAME MAY VARY DEPENDING ON THE PLATFORM AND THE PURPOSE OF THIS TOOL IS TO ALLOW YOU TO CHOOSE THE TYPE OF ANIMATION YOU ARE LOOKING FOR WITHIN A SERIES OF UNIQUE ARTISTIC STYLES LOADED ON THE PLATFORM BY DEFAULT TO HELP YOU OBTAIN A MORE ACCURATE RESULT.

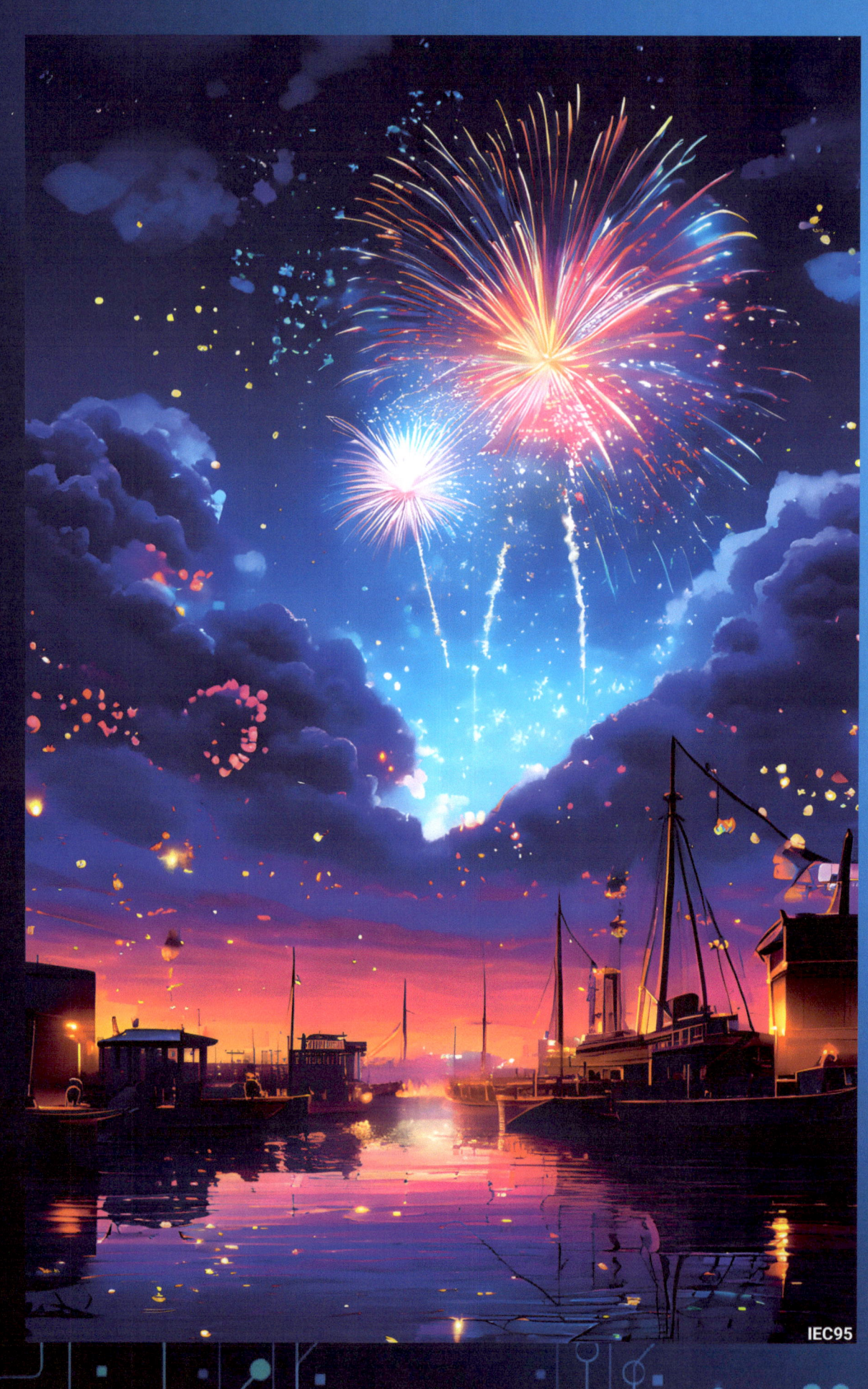
IEC95

1

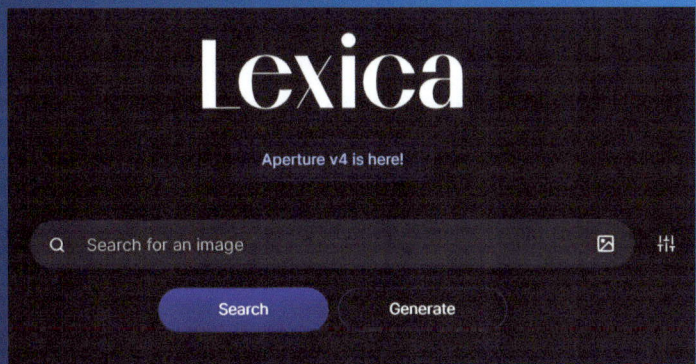

Lexica.art is a very easy-to-use artificial intelligence (AI) platform that will allow you to create up to a maximum of 100 free images per month or you can pay a subscription to be able to create unlimited images.

This platform employs advanced AI models such as Generative Adversarial Networks (GAN) to interpret and translate textual descriptions into detailed and realistic visual images. Users can provide text descriptions of scenes, objects, or concepts, and Lexica.art will generate corresponding images that creatively and accurately reflect those descriptions. This platform is useful for a wide range of applications, including graphic design, visual content creation, digital art production, and AI research.

INTERFACE TOOLS

IN THE UPPER RIGHT CORNER YOU WILL FIND THE "GET STARTED" BUTTON TO SIGN UP AND ENTER THE INTERFACE

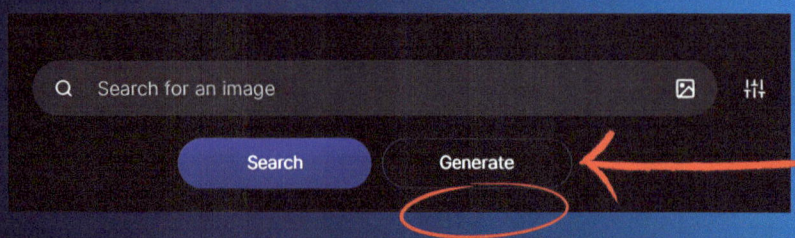

TO START CREATING YOUR IMAGES JUST HAVE TO PRESS THE "GENERATE" BUTTON

ONCE INSIDE THE CREATION INTERFACE YOU WILL FIND THE FOLLOWING ELEMENTS.

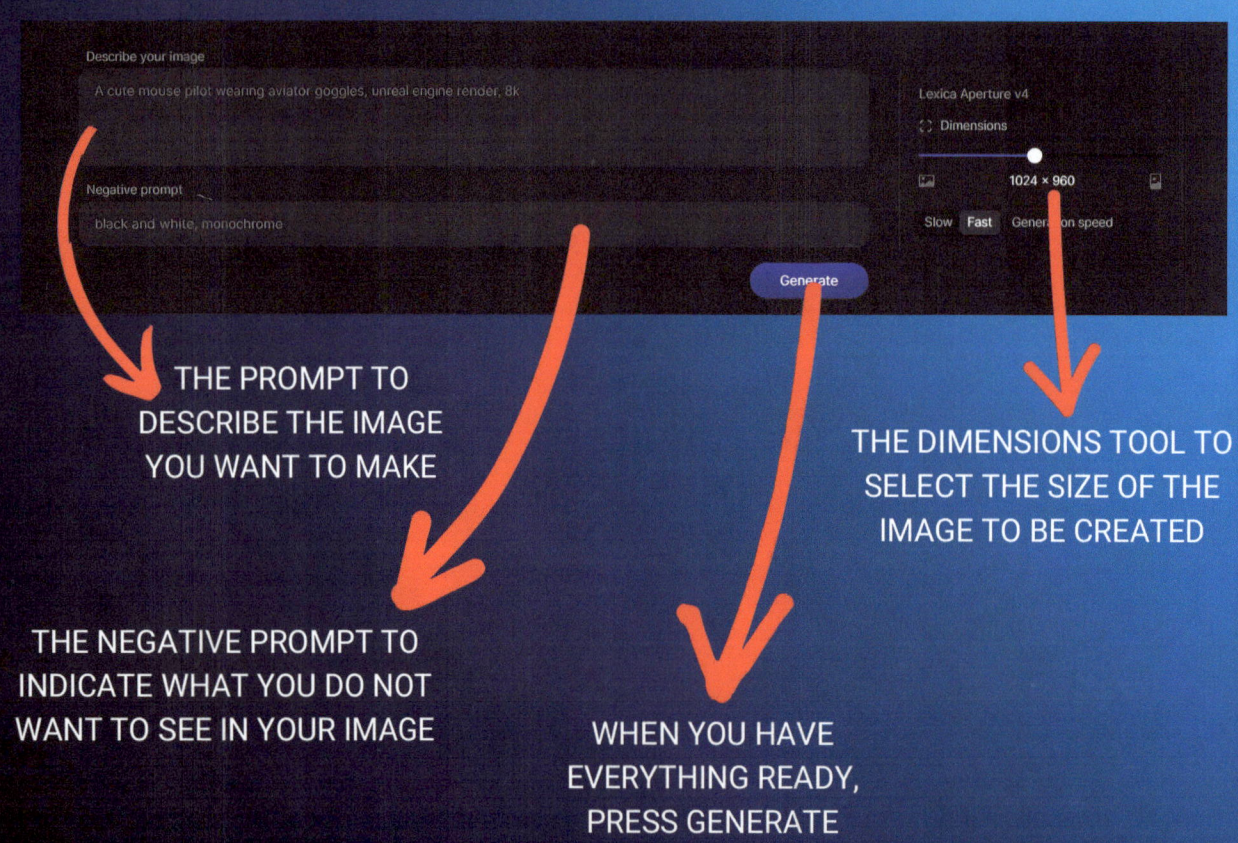

THE PROMPT TO DESCRIBE THE IMAGE YOU WANT TO MAKE

THE DIMENSIONS TOOL TO SELECT THE SIZE OF THE IMAGE TO BE CREATED

THE NEGATIVE PROMPT TO INDICATE WHAT YOU DO NOT WANT TO SEE IN YOUR IMAGE

WHEN YOU HAVE EVERYTHING READY, PRESS GENERATE

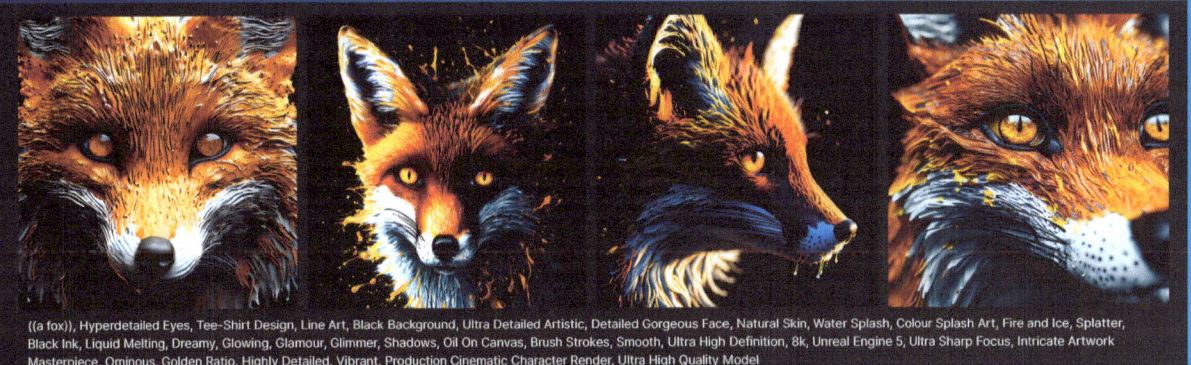

((a fox)), Hyperdetailed Eyes, Tee-Shirt Design, Line Art, Black Background, Ultra Detailed Artistic, Detailed Gorgeous Face, Natural Skin, Water Splash, Colour Splash Art, Fire and Ice, Splatter, Black Ink, Liquid Melting, Dreamy, Glowing, Glamour, Glimmer, Shadows, Oil On Canvas, Brush Strokes, Smooth, Ultra High Definition, 8k, Unreal Engine 5, Ultra Sharp Focus, Intricate Artwork Masterpiece, Ominous, Golden Ratio, Highly Detailed, Vibrant, Production Cinematic Character Render, Ultra High Quality Model

USING THE SPECIFICATIONS YOU WROTE, 4 IMAGES ARE CREATED SIMULTANEOUSLY AND BY MOVING THE CURSOR OVER ANY OF THEM YOU WILL BE ABLE TO DOWNLOAD THE SELECTED IMAGE WITHOUT ANY PROBLEMS, REMEMBER TO TRY TO BE AS SPECIFIC AS POSSIBLE REGARDING WHAT YOU WANT WHEN DESIGNING YOUR IMAGES.

YOU CAN ALSO VIEW THE CREATIONS OF OTHERS AND RECREATE THEIR WORK SIMPLY BY CLICKING OPEN IN EDITOR

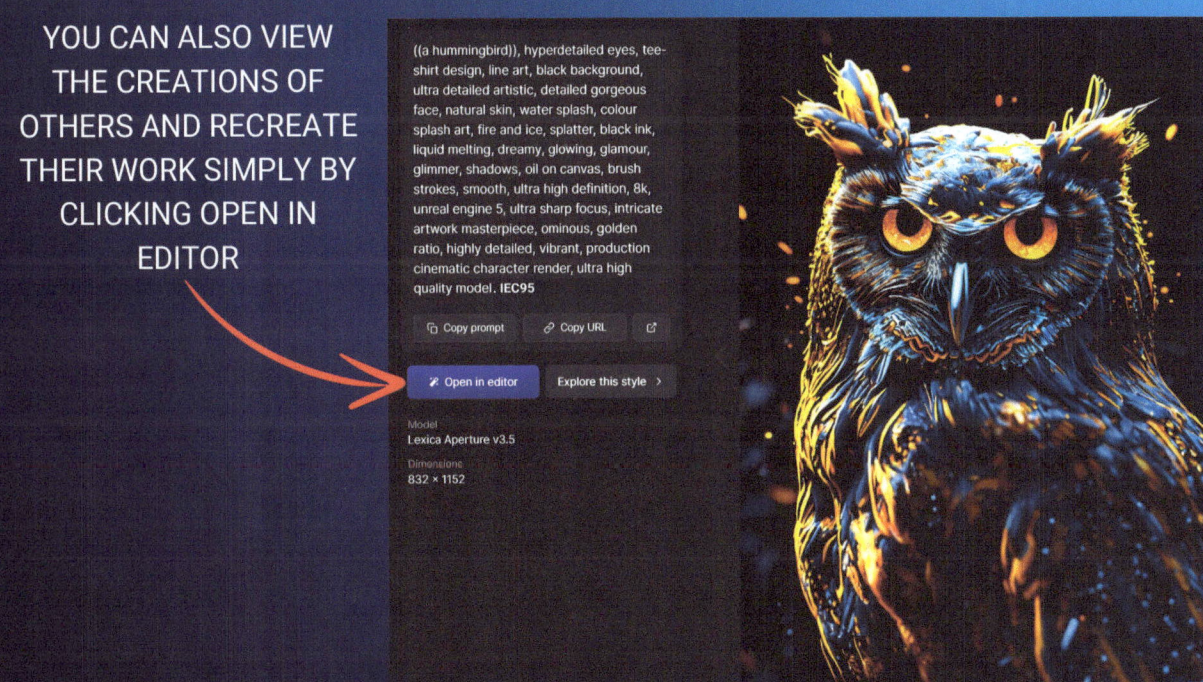

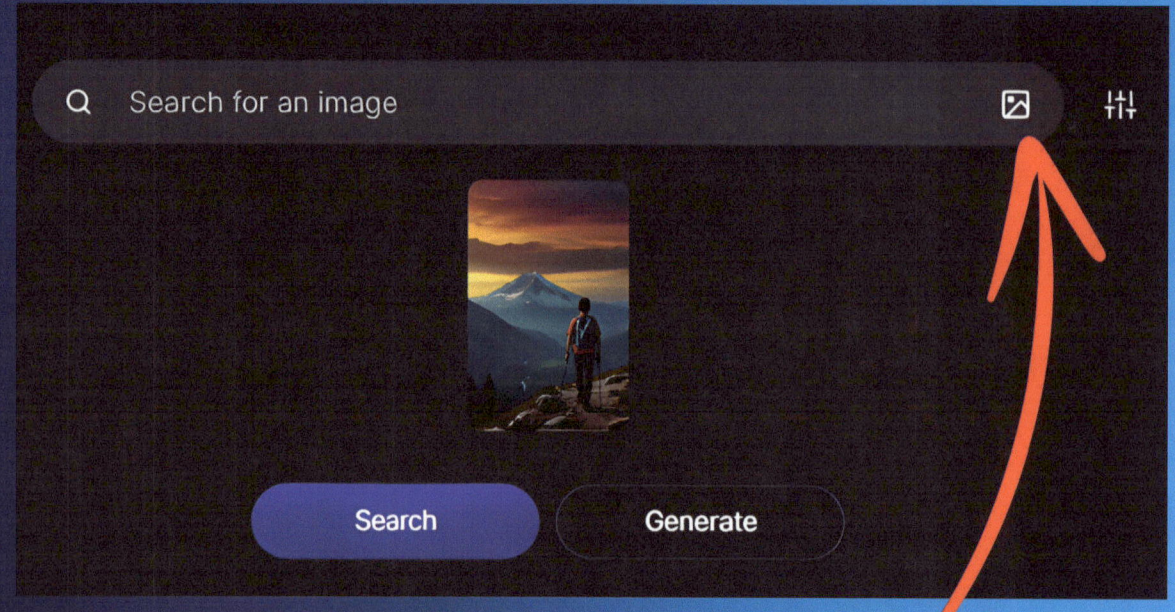

YOU CAN UPLOAD A REFERENCE IMAGE TO BE ABLE TO SEARCH FOR SIMILAR IMAGES THAT WERE CREATED BY THE COMMUNITY

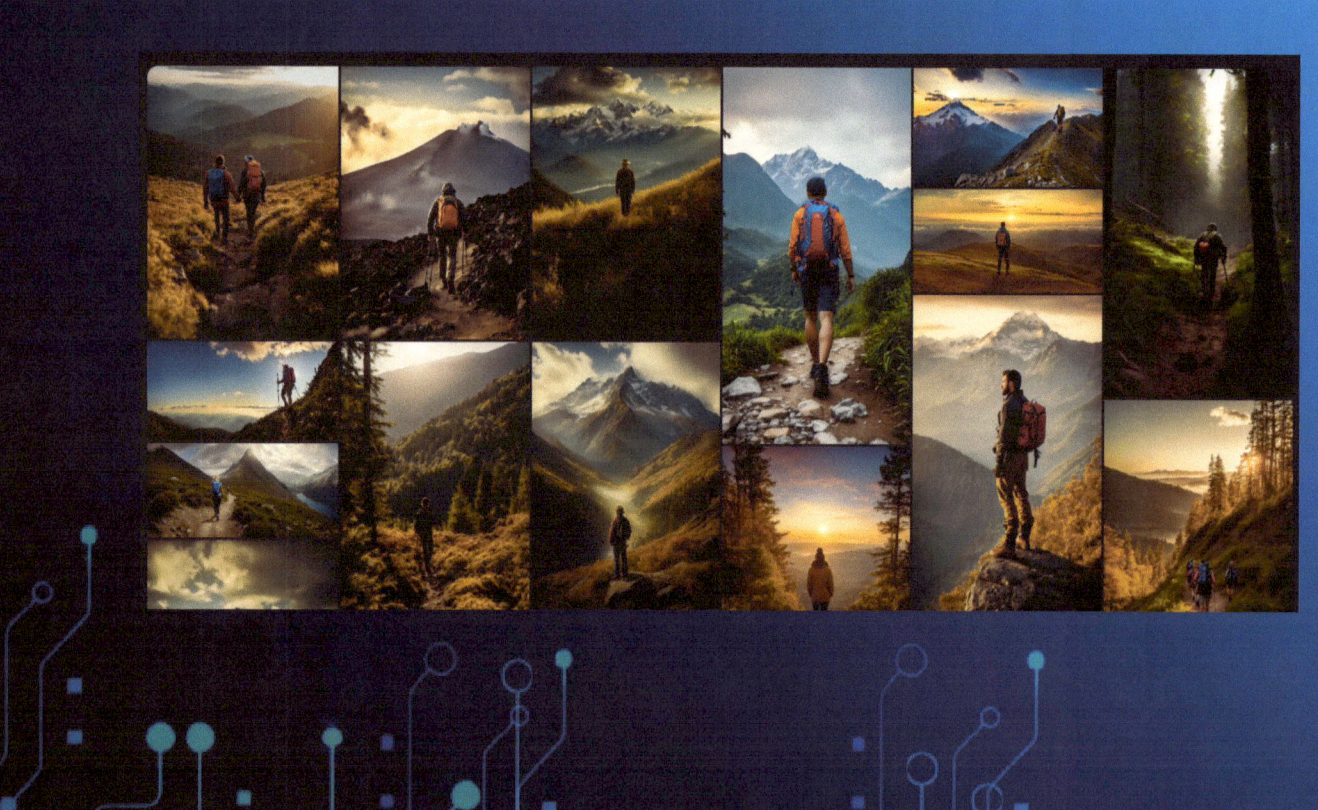

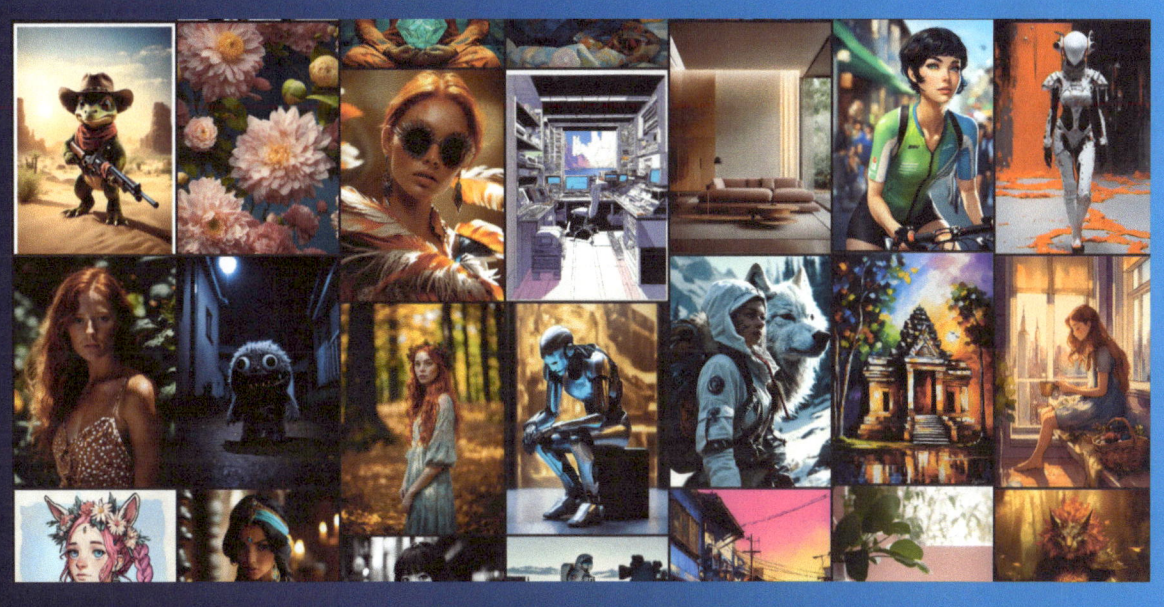

THE LEXICA COMMUNITY IS VERY
ACTIVE AND AT ALL TIMES YOU CAN
SEE OTHER PEOPLE'S WORK AND
MARVEL AT ALL THE THINGS THAT
CAN BE CREATED.

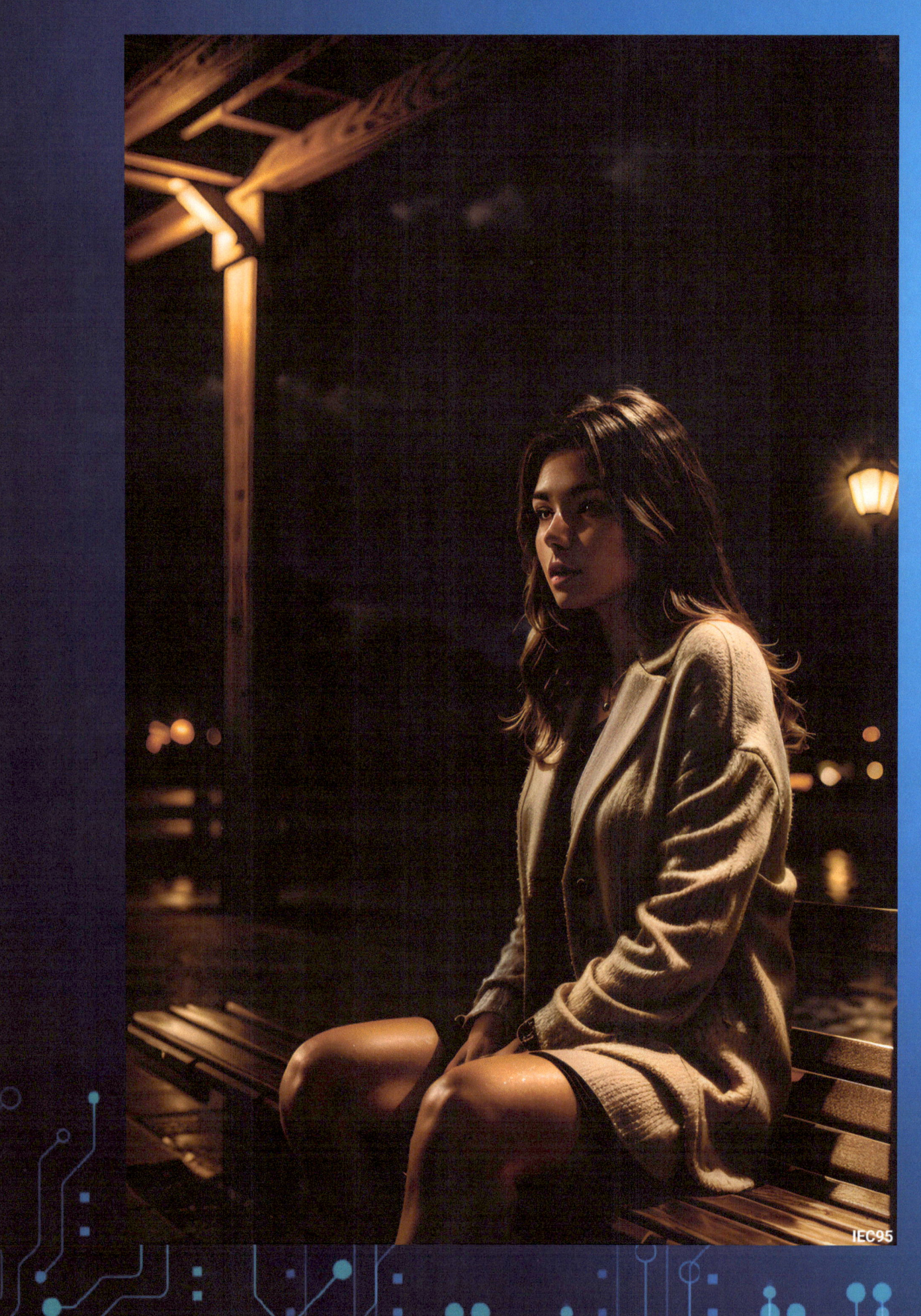
IEC95

2

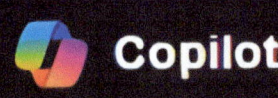

COPILOT DESIGNER IS AN ARTIFICIAL INTELLIGENCE CREATED BY THE COMPANY OPENAI. WHEN YOU ENTER THE PLATFORM YOU WILL HAVE TO REGISTER WITH A MICROSOFT ACCOUNT, WHEN YOU PRESS THE SIGN UP BUTTON YOU CAN CREATE ONE OR LOAD YOUR ACCOUNT IF YOU ALREADY HAVE ONE.

OPENAI IS AN ARTIFICIAL INTELLIGENCE RESEARCH COMPANY. IT WAS FOUNDED IN DECEMBER 2015 BY ELON MUSK, SAM ALTMAN, AND OTHER PROMINENT INVESTORS WITH THE GOAL OF PROMOTING AND DEVELOPING AI IN A SAFE AND BENEFICIAL MANNER FOR HUMANITY. OPENAI WORKS IN A VARIETY OF AI RESEARCH AREAS, INCLUDING DEEP LEARNING, ROBOTICS, NATURAL LANGUAGE PROCESSING, AND COMPUTATIONAL CREATIVITY.

INTERFACE TOOLS

ONCE YOU HAVE REGISTERED YOU WILL BE ABLE TO SEE THE FOLLOWING ELEMENTS

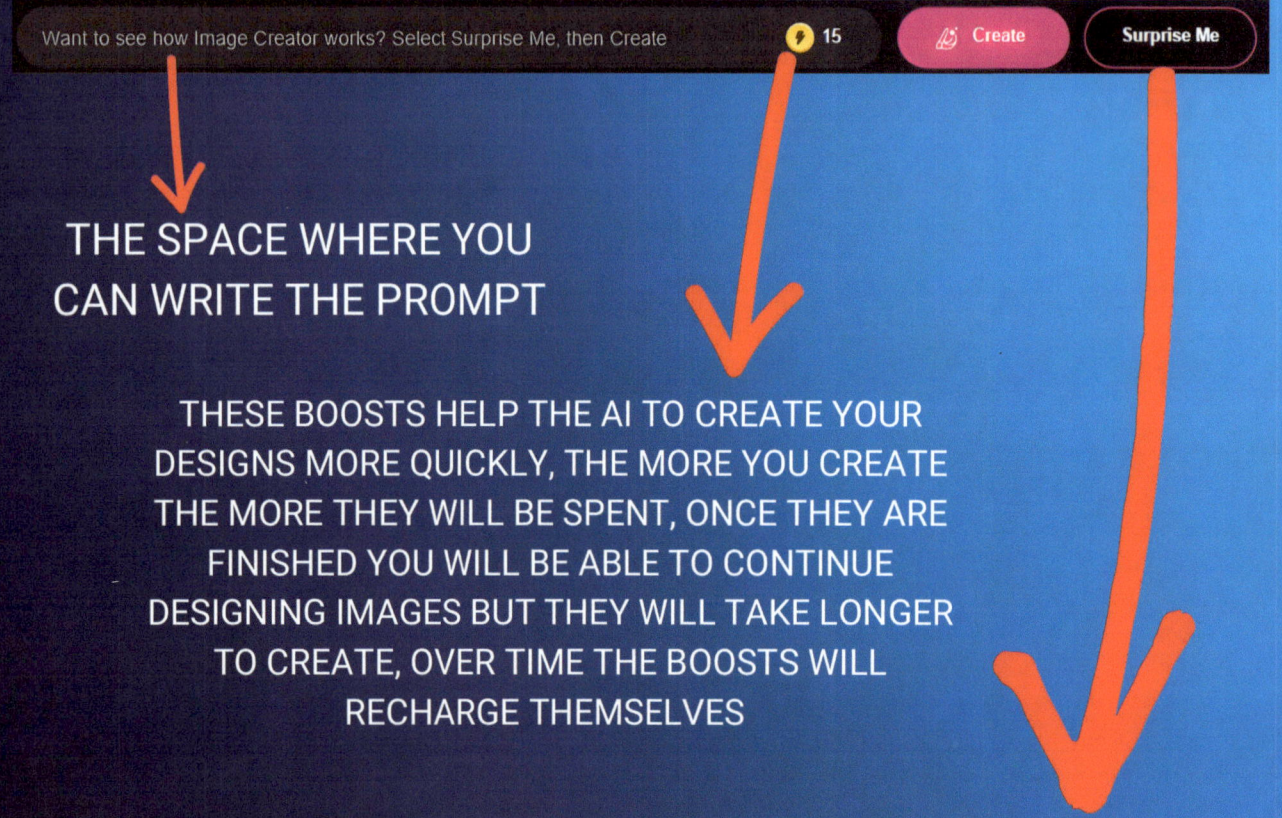

THE SPACE WHERE YOU
CAN WRITE THE PROMPT

THESE BOOSTS HELP THE AI TO CREATE YOUR
DESIGNS MORE QUICKLY, THE MORE YOU CREATE
THE MORE THEY WILL BE SPENT, ONCE THEY ARE
FINISHED YOU WILL BE ABLE TO CONTINUE
DESIGNING IMAGES BUT THEY WILL TAKE LONGER
TO CREATE, OVER TIME THE BOOSTS WILL
RECHARGE THEMSELVES

THE SURPRISE ME BUTTON WHEN PRESSED
GENERATES A RANDOM PROMPT SO YOU CAN
EXPLORE THE CAPABILITIES OF THIS AI

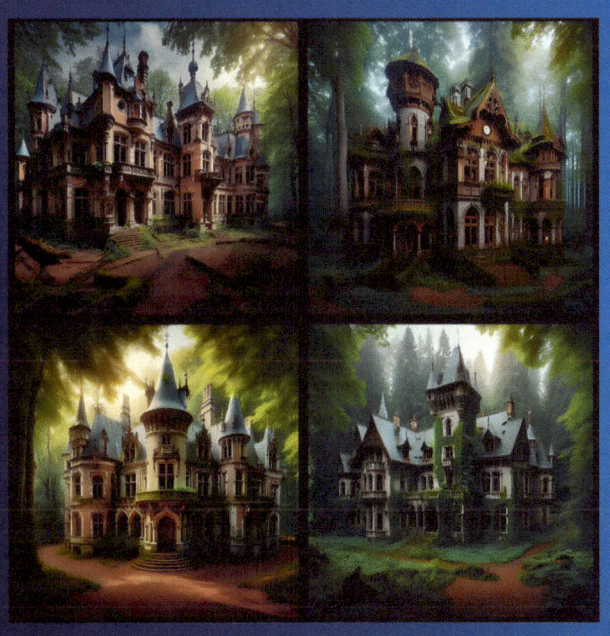

IN COPILOT YOU CANNOT CHANGE THE DIMENSIONS OF THE IMAGES SO 4 IMAGES WILL BE CREATED SIMULTANEOUSLY IN A STANDARD SIZE OF 1024 X 1024 AND BY SELECTING ANY OF THEM YOU CAN DOWNLOAD IT

ALL IMAGES CREATED ARE SAVED IN A GALLERY WHERE YOU CAN STORE THEM FOR A MAXIMUM OF 90 DAYS

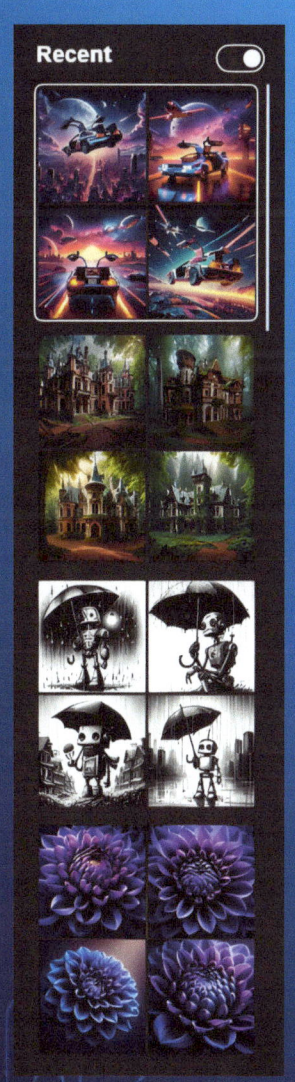

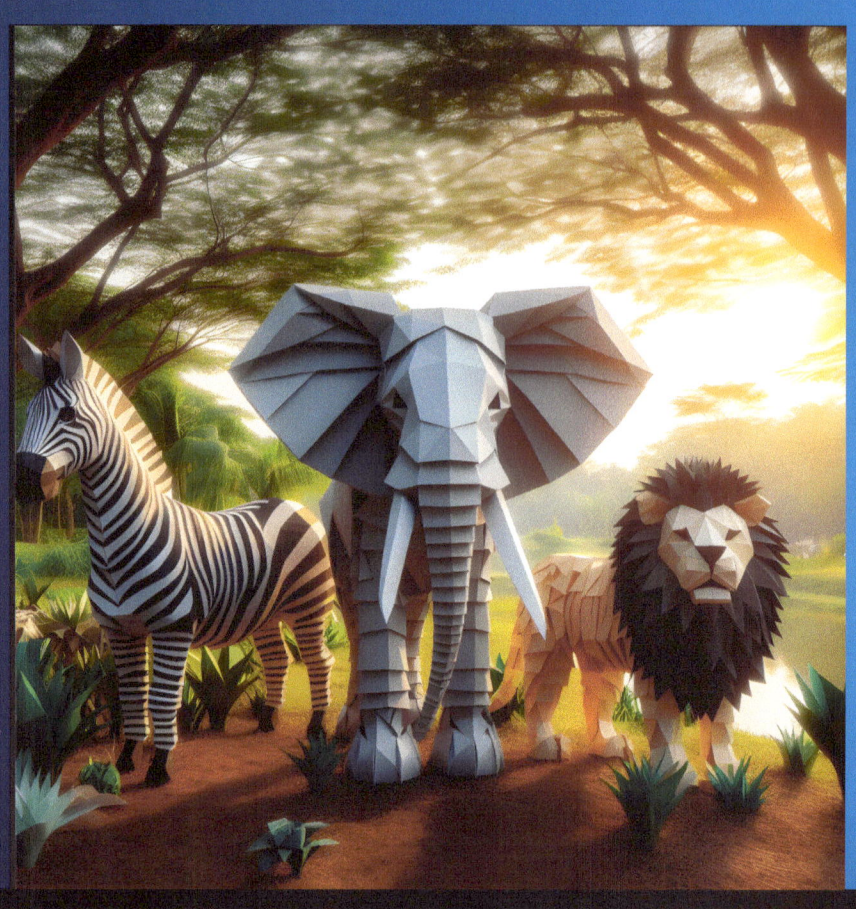

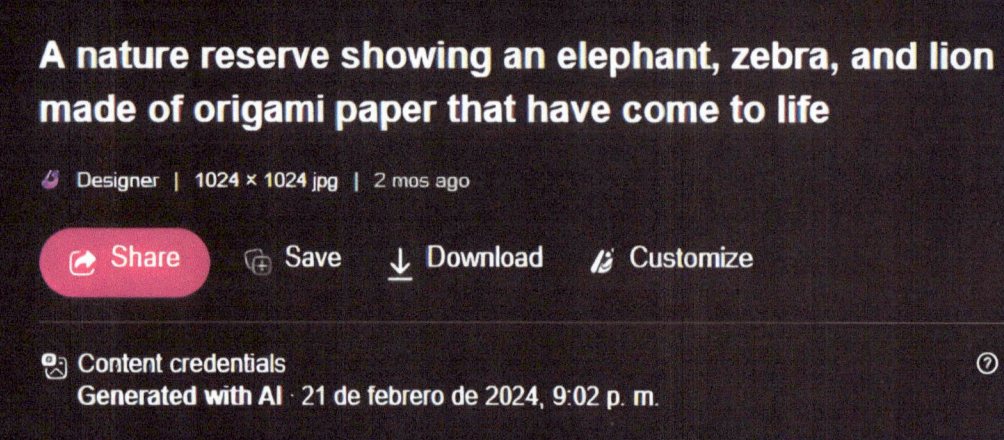

A nature reserve showing an elephant, zebra, and lion made of origami paper that have come to life

Designer | 1024 × 1024 jpg | 2 mos ago

Share   Save   Download   Customize

Content credentials
Generated with AI · 21 de febrero de 2024, 9:02 p. m.

YOU WILL BE ABLE TO SEE SOME IMAGES CREATED IN COPILOT WHICH YOU CAN DOWNLOAD OR COPY THE PROMPT.

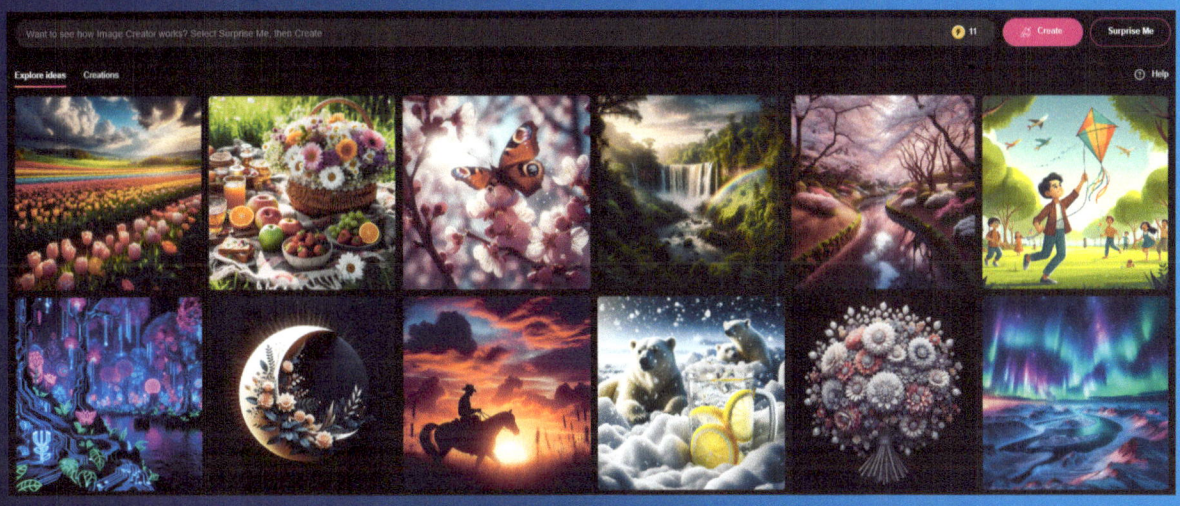

FROM THE FIRST MOMENT YOU REGISTER, COPILOT WILL WELCOME YOU WITH SOME ILLUSTRATIONS THAT YOU CAN RECREATE OR BE INSPIRED BY TO CREATE YOUR OWN ORIGINAL IMAGES.

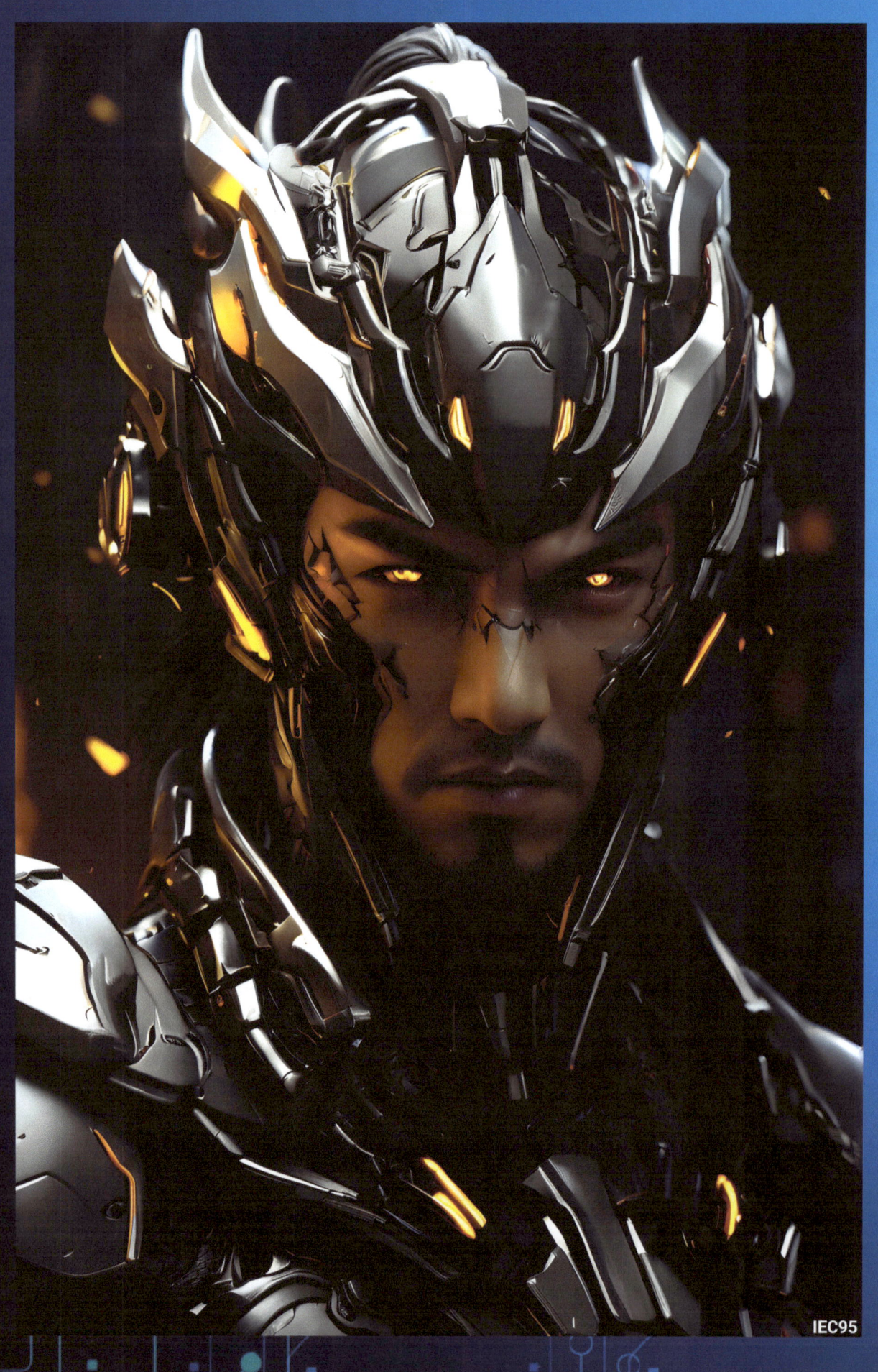

IEC95

3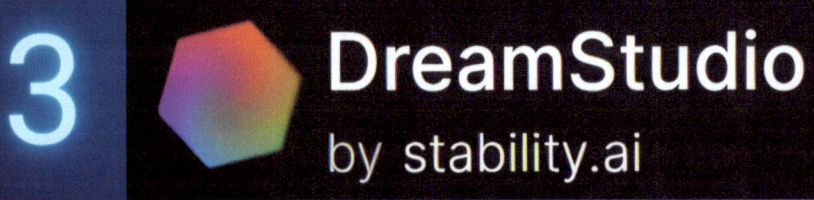

DREAMSTUDIO IS AN ARTIFICIAL INTELLIGENCE PLATFORM THAT PROVIDES A USER-FRIENDLY AND ACCESSIBLE INTERFACE FOR CREATING IMAGES AND VISUAL CONTENT. UPON REGISTRATION, USERS RECEIVE AN INITIAL ALLOCATION OF CREDITS, WHICH THEY CAN USE TO GENERATE A VARIETY OF IMAGES. ONCE THESE CREDITS ARE DEPLETED, USERS HAVE THE OPTION TO ACQUIRE MORE THROUGH A PAYMENT SYSTEM, ALLOWING THEM TO CONTINUE USING THE PLATFORM SEAMLESSLY AND WITHOUT INTERRUPTION.

IN THE UPPER RIGHT CORNER YOU WILL FIND THE "LOGIN" BUTTON TO SIGN UP

Login

INTERFACE TOOLS

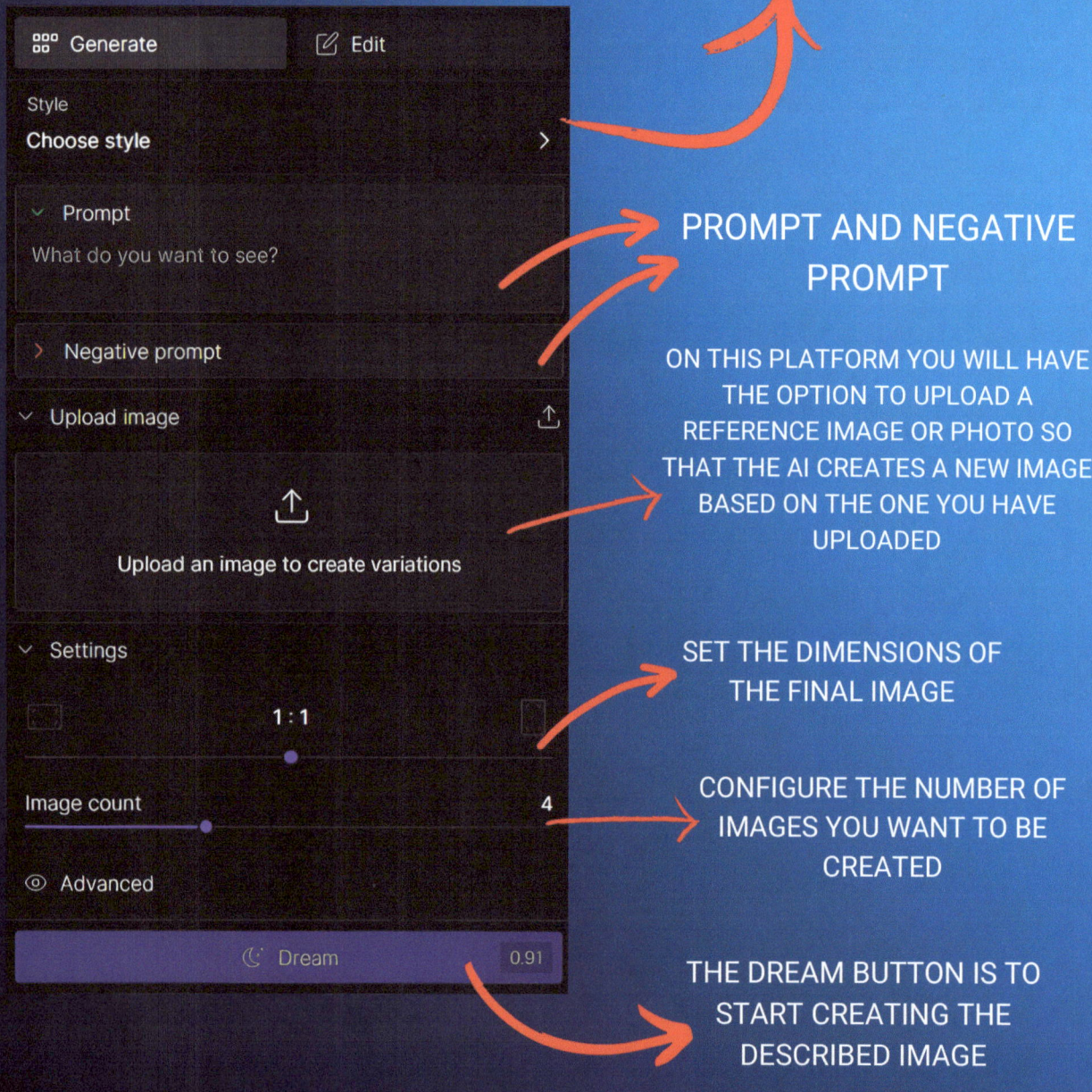

CHOOSE STYLE HELPS YOU BE MORE PRECISE ABOUT THE ANIMATION STYLE YOU ARE LOOKING FOR.

PROMPT AND NEGATIVE PROMPT

ON THIS PLATFORM YOU WILL HAVE THE OPTION TO UPLOAD A REFERENCE IMAGE OR PHOTO SO THAT THE AI CREATES A NEW IMAGE BASED ON THE ONE YOU HAVE UPLOADED

SET THE DIMENSIONS OF THE FINAL IMAGE

CONFIGURE THE NUMBER OF IMAGES YOU WANT TO BE CREATED

THE DREAM BUTTON IS TO START CREATING THE DESCRIBED IMAGE

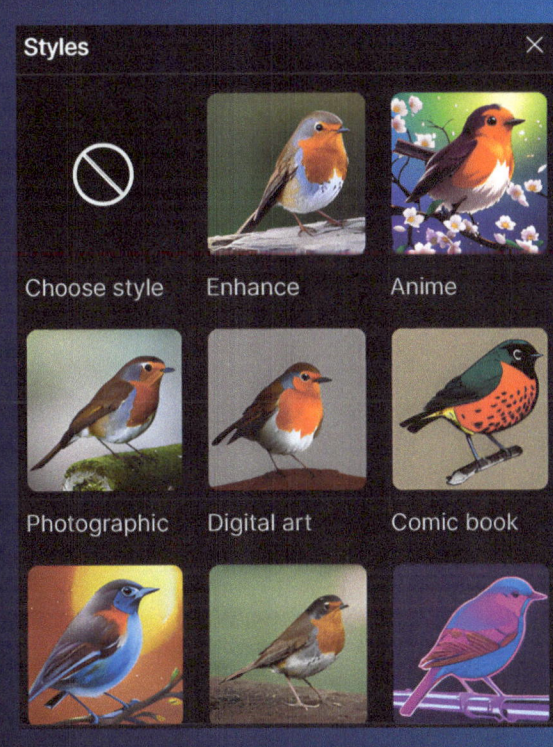

WITH THE CHOOSE STYLE YOU COULD OBTAIN DIFFERENT RESULTS FROM THE SAME PROMPT AND THUS SPEED UP THE WORK A LITTLE IN TERMS OF SEARCHING FOR THE ARTISTIC DESIGN YOU ARE LOOKING FOR.

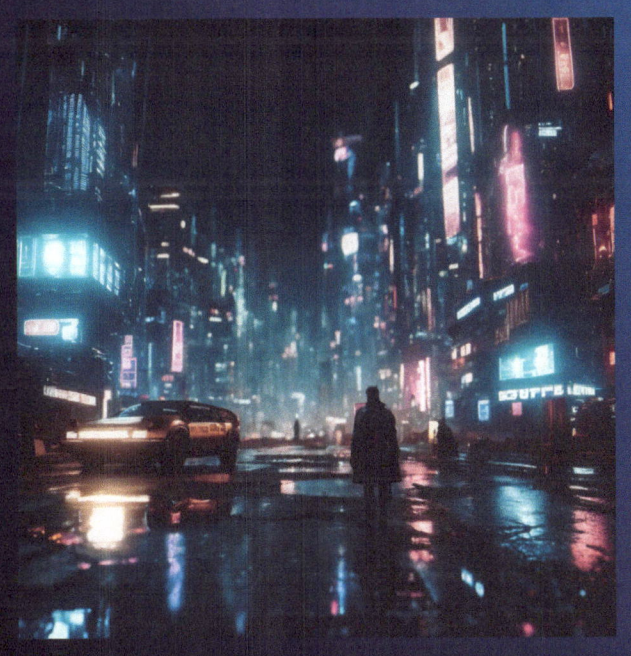

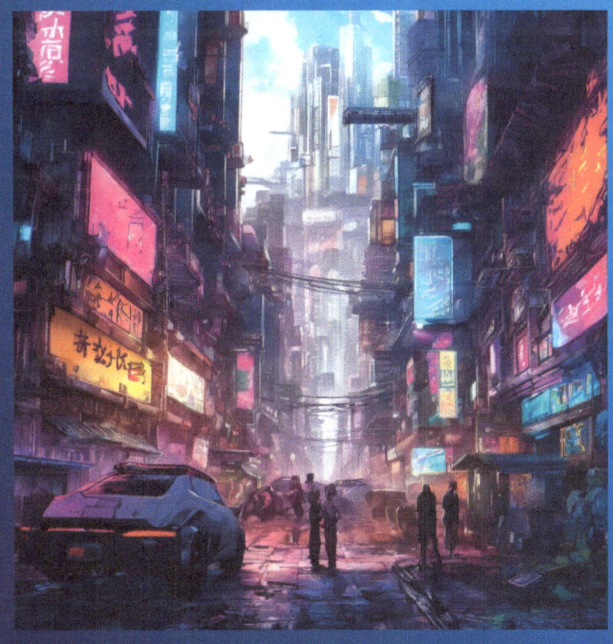

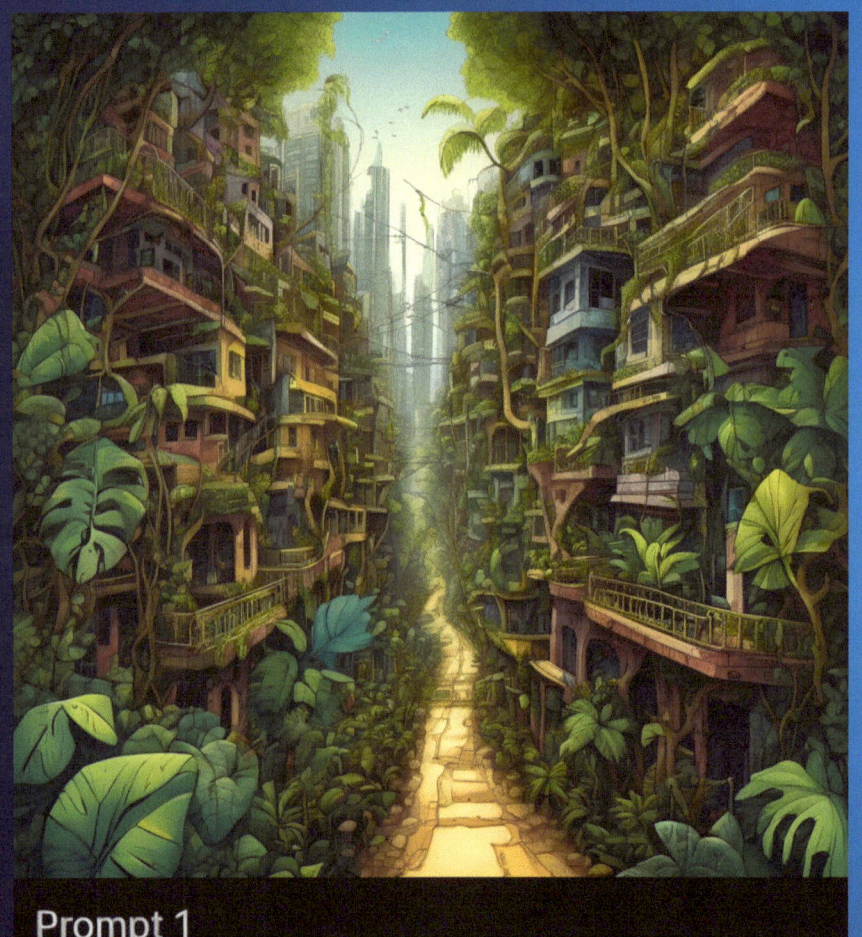

Prompt 1

A jungle city, with vines and roots serving as roads and buildings made of leaves, colorful, detailed, natural, tropical

stable-diffusion-xl-1024-v1-0

Ratio 1 : 1   Size 1024 × 1024

Seed 918861   Steps 40

WHEN THE IMAGES ARE CREATED YOU CAN DOWNLOAD THEM WITHOUT ANY PROBLEMS

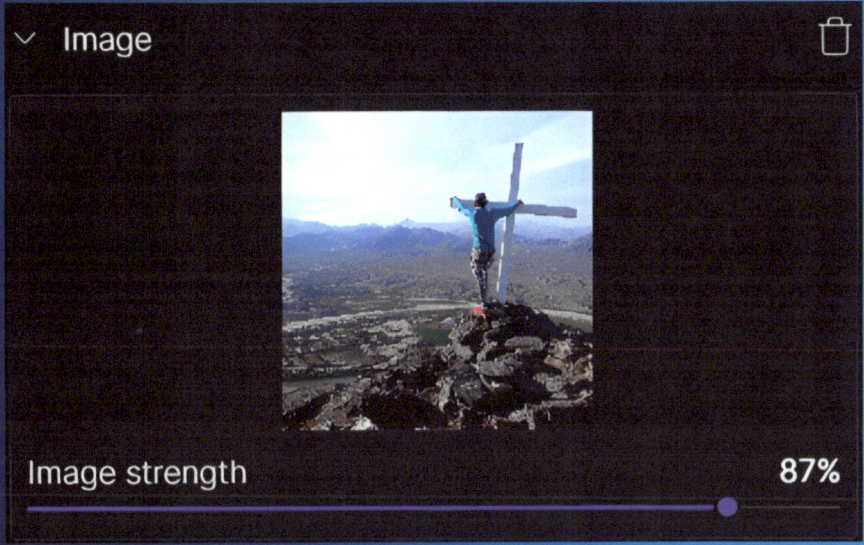

Image strength 87%

WHEN LOADING A REFERENCE IMAGE, THE IMAGE INTENSITY OPTION APPEARS. BY RAISING THE PERCENTAGE WE WILL BE TELLING THE AI TO CREATE AN IMAGE AS SIMILAR AS POSSIBLE TO THE REFERENCE IMAGE AND IF WE LOWER THE PERCENTAGE WE WILL BE ALLOWING THE AI TO TAKE MORE CREATIVE FREEDOM REGARDING THE FINAL RESULT.

IT IS ADVISABLE TO ADD A PROMPT DESCRIBING THE UPLOADED IMAGE TO HELP THE AI UNDERSTAND THE CONTENT OF THE IMAGE MORE CLEARLY.

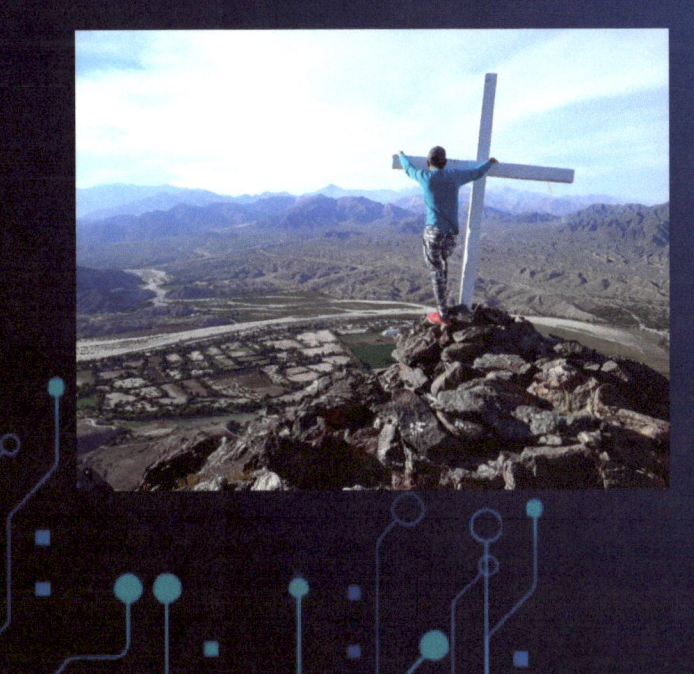
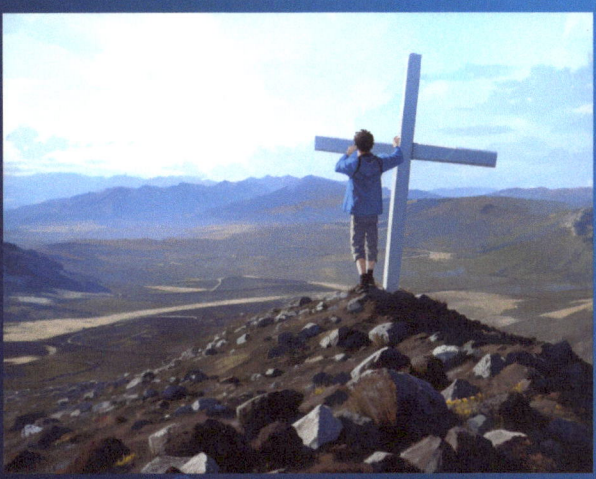

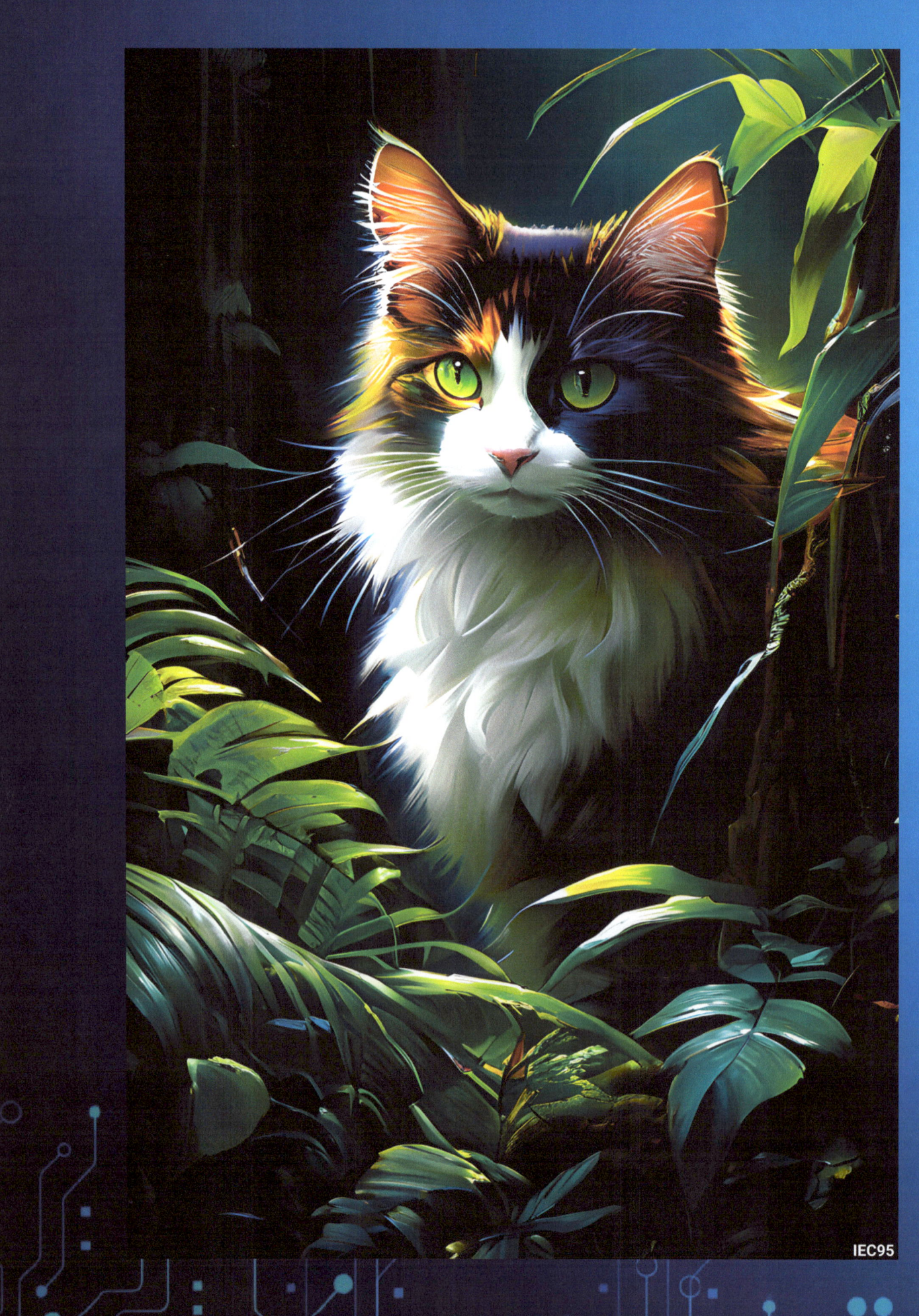

IEC95

4 TensorArt

TENSOR.ART IS AN ARTIFICIAL
INTELLIGENCE PLATFORM THAT WORKS
WITH A CREDIT PURCHASE SYSTEM BUT
WHEN YOU REGISTER YOU WILL BE
GRANTED 100 DAILY CREDITS FOR THE
CREATION OF IMAGES AND NOT JUST
IMAGES SINCE ON THIS PLATFORM YOU
CAN CREATE ANIMATIONS ACCORDING TO
YOUR INSTRUCTIONS AND YOU CAN ALSO
UPLOAD YOUR OWN PHOTOS AND
REFERENCE IMAGES TO RECREATE THEM TO
YOUR LIKING.

IN THE UPPER RIGHT CORNER YOU WILL FIND THE "SIGN IN"
BUTTON FOR YOU TO REGISTER LUEGO JUST CLICK ON THE
CREATE BUTTON TO START DESIGNING YOUR IMAGES.

Sign In

Search 🔍 ✨ Create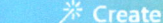

INTERFACE TOOLS

CREATE IMAGES

CREATE ANIMATION

UPLOAD IMAGES

PROMPT
AND
NEGATIVE
PROMPT

CHOOSE A MODEL
WITH THE
ANIMATION STYLE
YOU ARE LOOKING
FOR BEFORE YOU
START

ADD MORE
THAN ONE
MODEL

PERFORM
COLOR
CORRECTIONS

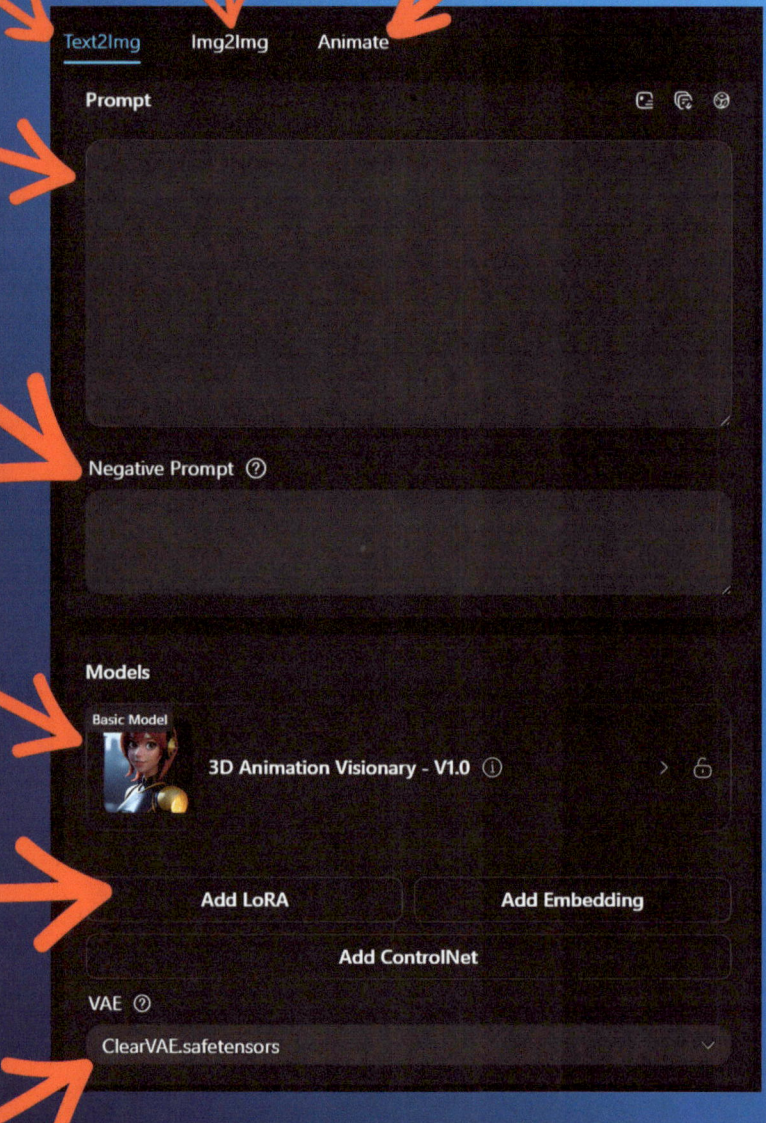

FINAL IMAGE DIMENSIONS

TO GET DIFFERENT RESULTS FROM THE SAME PROMPT

TO INCREASE OR DECREASE THE AMOUNT OF INTERACTION THAT THE AI HAS TO REFINE THE IMAGE, RECOMMENDED FROM 10 TO 25

TO INCREASE OR DECREASE THE ACCURACY OF THE IMAGE WITH THE DESCRIPTION, RECOMMENDED FROM 3 TO 15

TO FURTHER REFINE THE FINAL RESULT, BUT WITH THE FREE VERSION ONLY LEAVE IT AT 1X AND DO NOT CHANGE THE REST OF THE OPTIONS

THE NUMBER OF IMAGES YOU WANT TO GENERATE

WHEN EVERYTHING IS READY, CLICK THE GENERATE BUTTON AND DEPENDING ON THE CONFIGURATION IT MAY CONSUME MORE OR LESS CREDITS

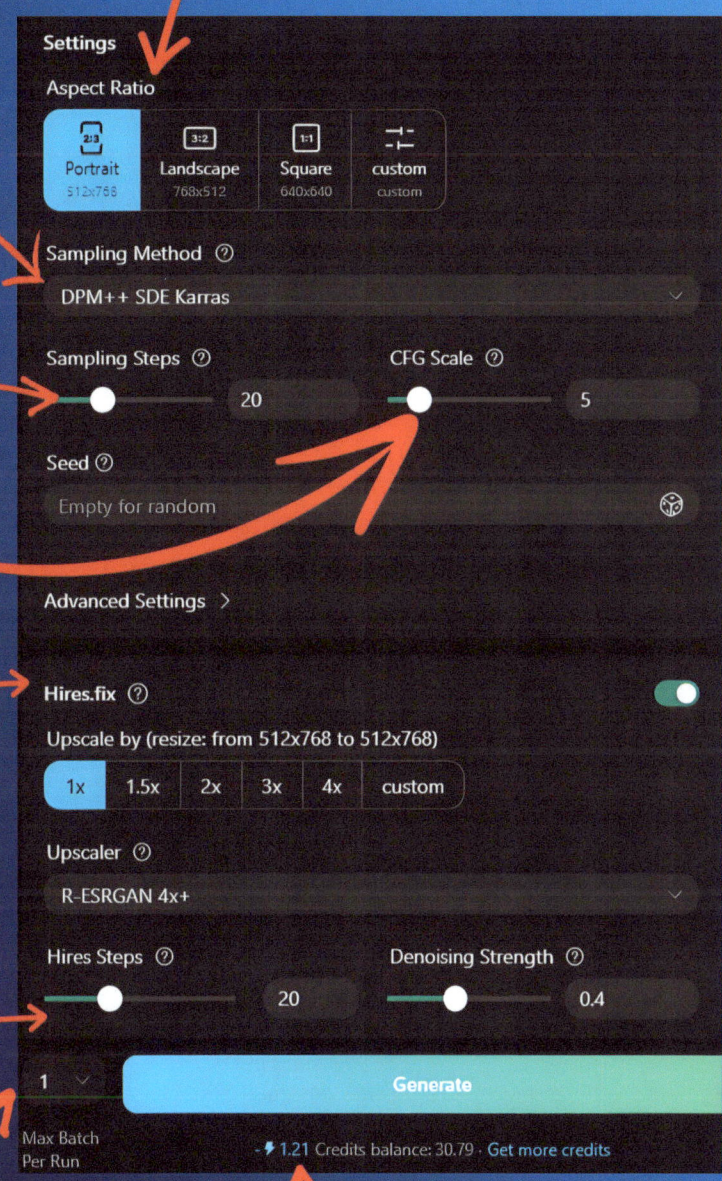

IN THE SECTION TO CREATE YOUR ANIMATION, THE SAME
TOOLS AS THE IMAGE CREATION INTERFACE WILL BE USED,
AND IN THE UPLOAD IMAGE SECTION, THE ONLY 2 NEW
TOOLS YOU WILL FIND ARE:

UPLOAD IMAGE

Text2Img   Img2Img   Animate

Click or drag a file to this area to upload

STRENGTH TOOL

Settings

Denoising Strength ?

0.5

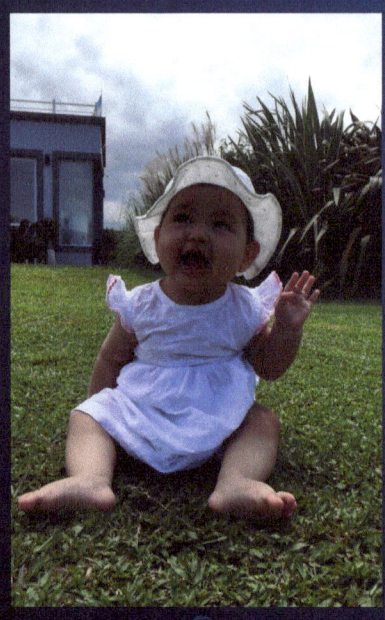
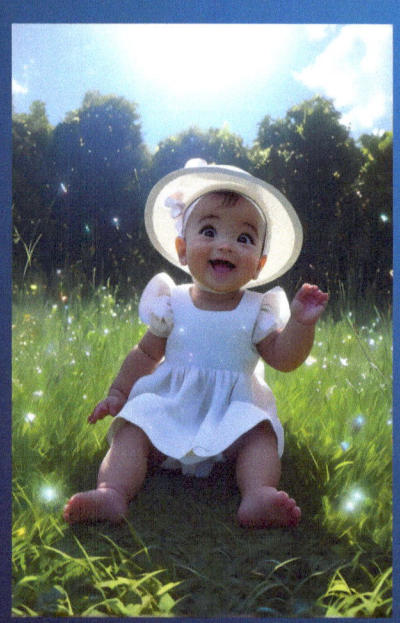

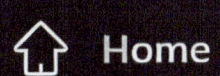

Home

AI Tools

Models

Posts

Leaderboard

IN THE POSTS SECTION YOU CAN SEE THE WORK DONE BY OTHER PEOPLE.

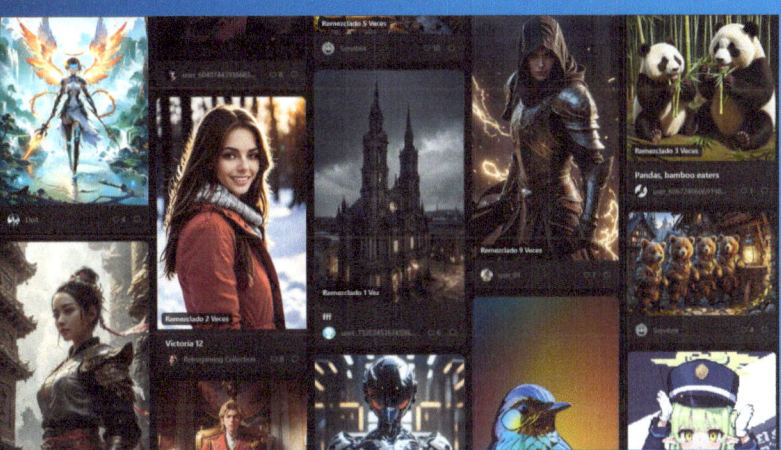

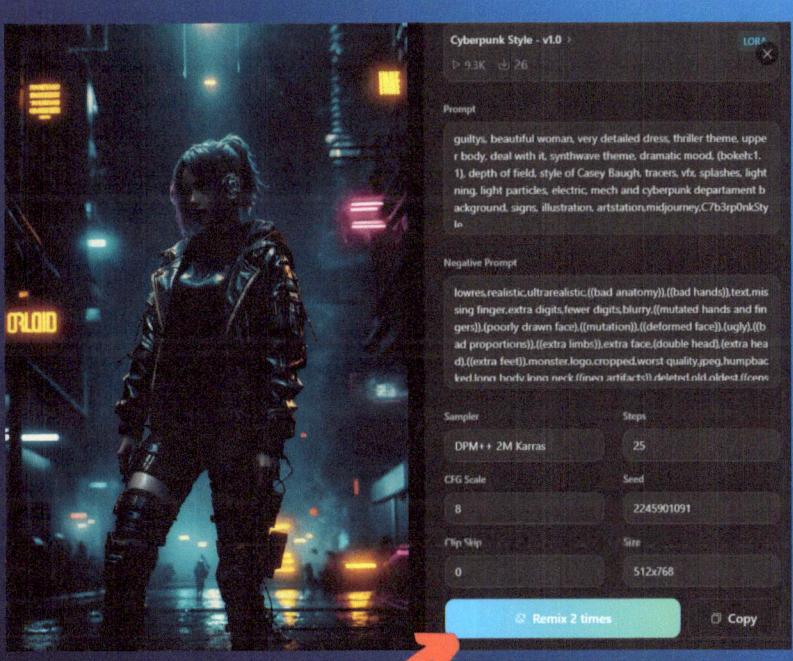

WHEN YOU SELECT AN IMAGE YOU WILL FIND THE REMIX BUTTON THAT, WHEN PRESSED, WILL TAKE YOU TO YOUR WORKSPACE WITH THE SETTINGS READY FOR YOU TO CREATE YOUR OWN VERSION OF THAT IMAGE.

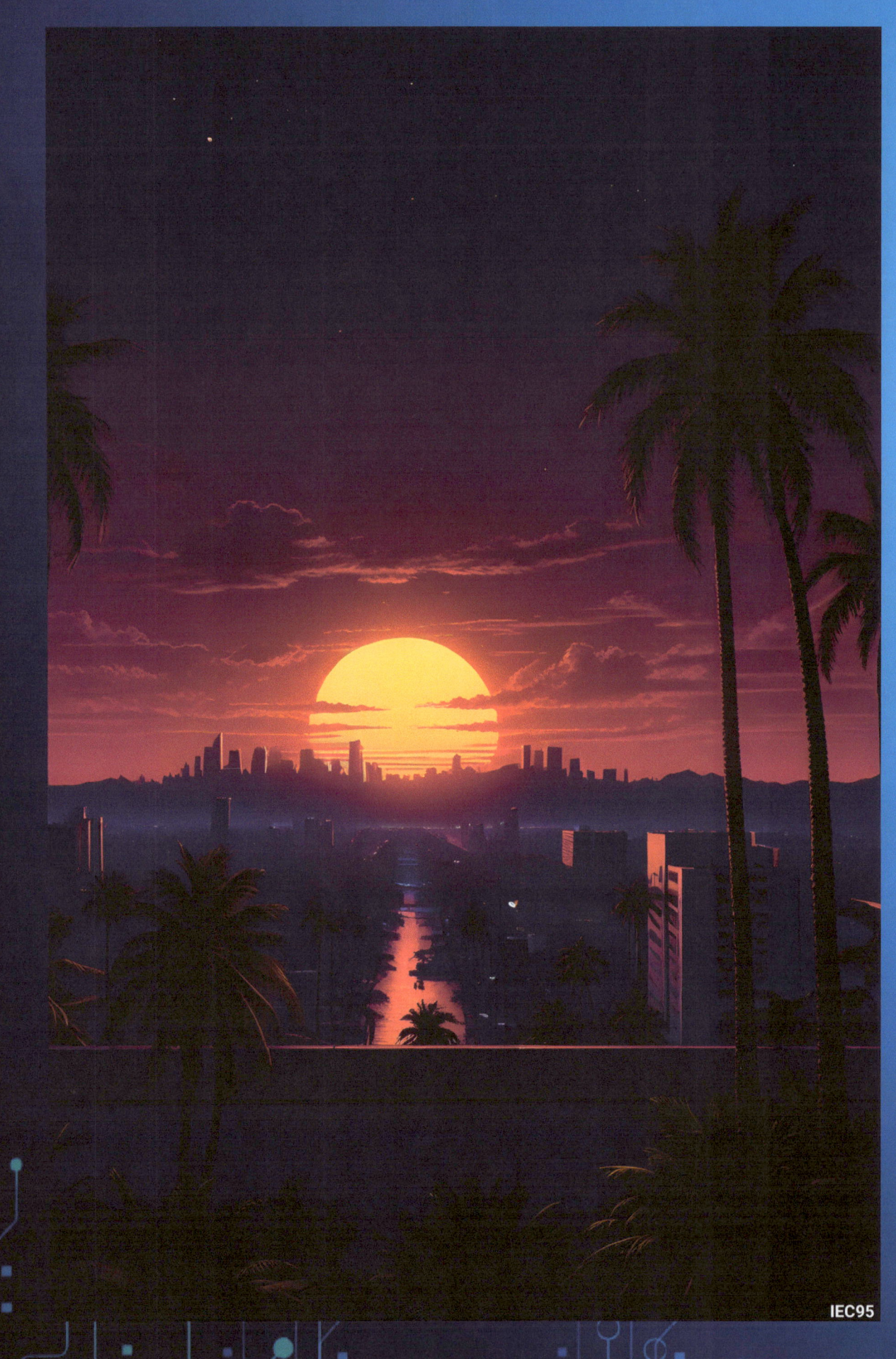

IEC95

5 ◐ Playground

PLAYGROUND AI IS AN ARTIFICIAL INTELLIGENCE PLATFORM IN WHICH WHEN YOU SIGN UP YOU CAN USE A FREE VERSION IN WHICH IT WILL ALLOW YOU TO CREATE UP TO 50 IMAGES DAILY OR PAY A SUBSCRIPTION TO GET A PRO VERSION WITH MANY MORE BENEFITS.

ONCE INSIDE THE PLATFORM YOU WILL FIND THE CREATE BUTTON TO START DESIGNING YOUR IMAGES

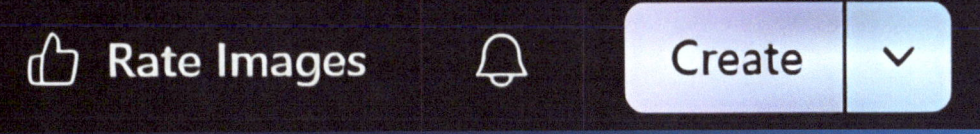

INTERFACE TOOLS

Image to Image ⊘

Upload or select an image to use as inspiration.

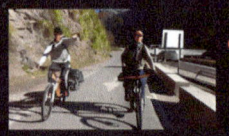

UPLOAD A REFERENCE IMAGE OR PHOTO

Image Strength

100

Image strength of 100 will generate the same image.

IMAGE STRENGTH

Filter ⊘

Experiment with different styles that can be applied to your image.

 Delicate detail ⌄

CHOOSE A MODEL OR ANIMATION STYLE ACCORDING TO WHAT YOU ARE LOOKING FOR

Expand Prompt ●

Use AI to improve short prompts and get new image style ideas.

Exclude From Image

Describe details you don't want in your image like colors, scenery, objects.

ugly, deformed, noisy, blurry, distorted, out of focus, bad anatomy, extra limbs, poorly drawn face, poorly drawn hands, missing fingers, nudity, nude

NEGATIVE PROMPT

DESIGNATES THE SIZE OF THE FINAL IMAGE

DESIGNATE THE NUMBER OF IMAGES YOU WANT TO CREATE

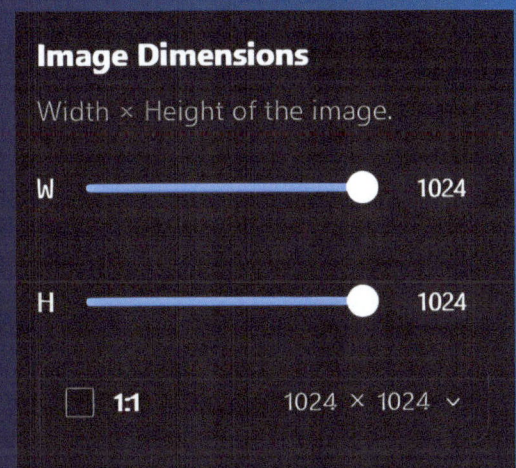

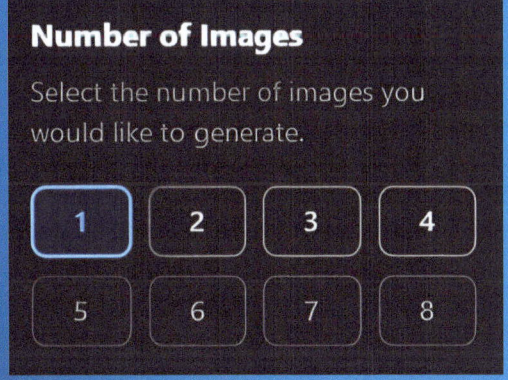

IN THE CENTER OF THE SCREEN YOU CAN FIND THE IMAGE FRAME AND BELOW THERE IS A SPACE TO PLACE THE PROMPT, WHEN DOWNLOADING YOU JUST HAVE TO PRESS THE DOWNLOAD OPTION THAT IS AT THE TOP OF THE CREATED IMAGE, ALL THE SPACE AROUND THE FRAME WILL FUNCTION AS A GALLERY WHERE YOU CAN MOVE AND ORGANIZE YOUR IMAGES AS YOU WISH.

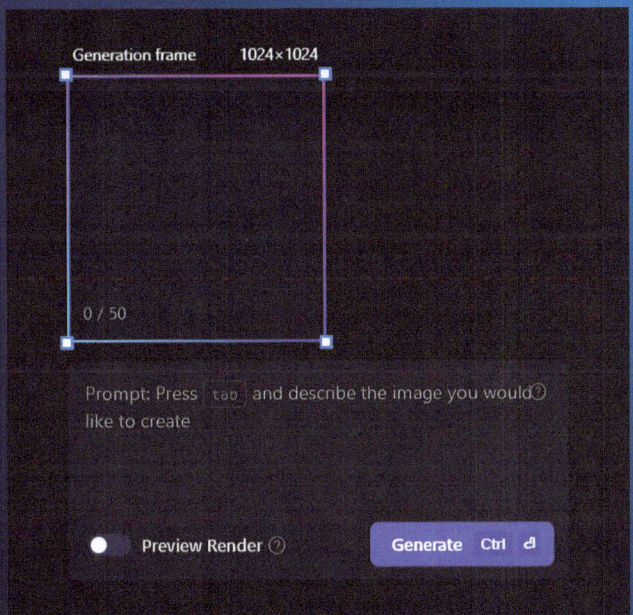

HOLD CNTL + MOUSE SCROLL TO ZOOM AND
HOLD SPACE + LEFT CLICK TO MOVE

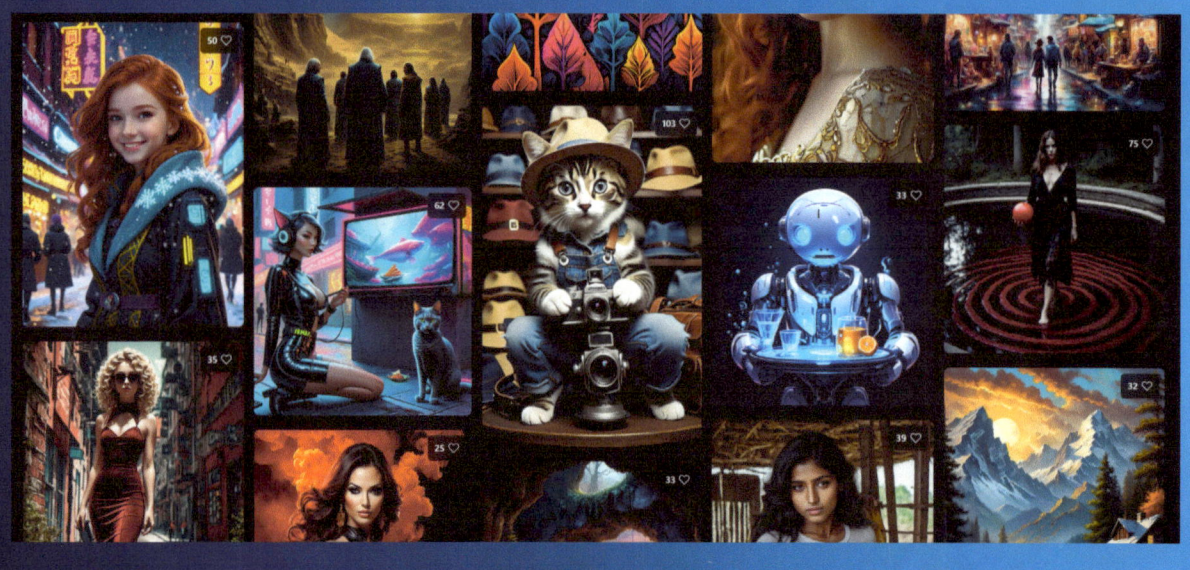

WHEN YOU ENTER THE
PLAYGROUND PLATFORM YOU
WILL BE ABLE TO SEE ALL THE
IMAGES CREATED BY ITS
COMMUNITY

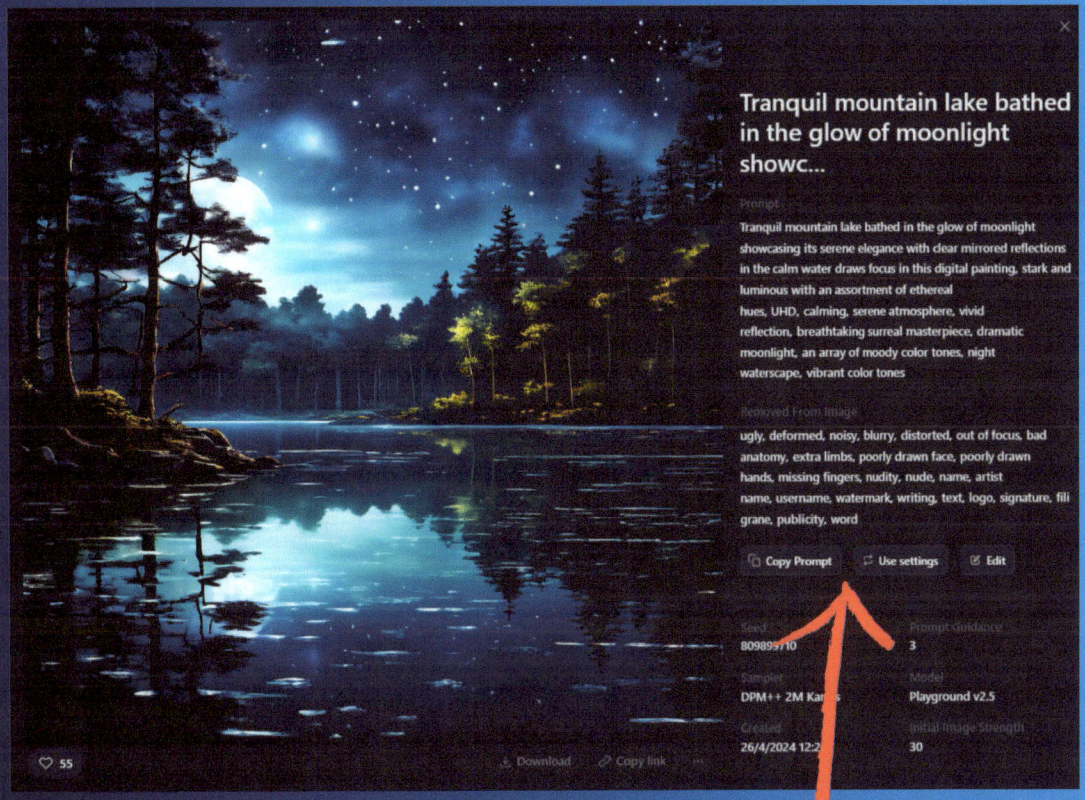

Tranquil mountain lake bathed in the glow of moonlight showc...

Prompt

Tranquil mountain lake bathed in the glow of moonlight showcasing its serene elegance with clear mirrored reflections in the calm water draws focus in this digital painting, stark and luminous with an assortment of ethereal hues, UHD, calming, serene atmosphere, vivid reflection, breathtaking surreal masterpiece, dramatic moonlight, an array of moody color tones, night waterscape, vibrant color tones

Removed From Image

ugly, deformed, noisy, blurry, distorted, out of focus, bad anatomy, extra limbs, poorly drawn face, poorly drawn hands, missing fingers, nudity, nude, name, artist name, username, watermark, writing, text, logo, signature, fili grane, publicity, word

Copy Prompt Use settings Edit

Seed | Prompt Guidance
809899710 | 3

Sampler | Model
DPM++ 2M Karras | Playground v2.5

Created | Initial Image Strength
26/4/2024 12:2 | 30

♡ 55   Download   Copy link

BY CLICKING ON AN IMAGE FROM ANOTHER
CREATOR YOU CAN COPY THE PROMPT OR USE
ALL ITS SETTINGS TO CREATE YOUR OWN
VERSION OF THE IMAGE

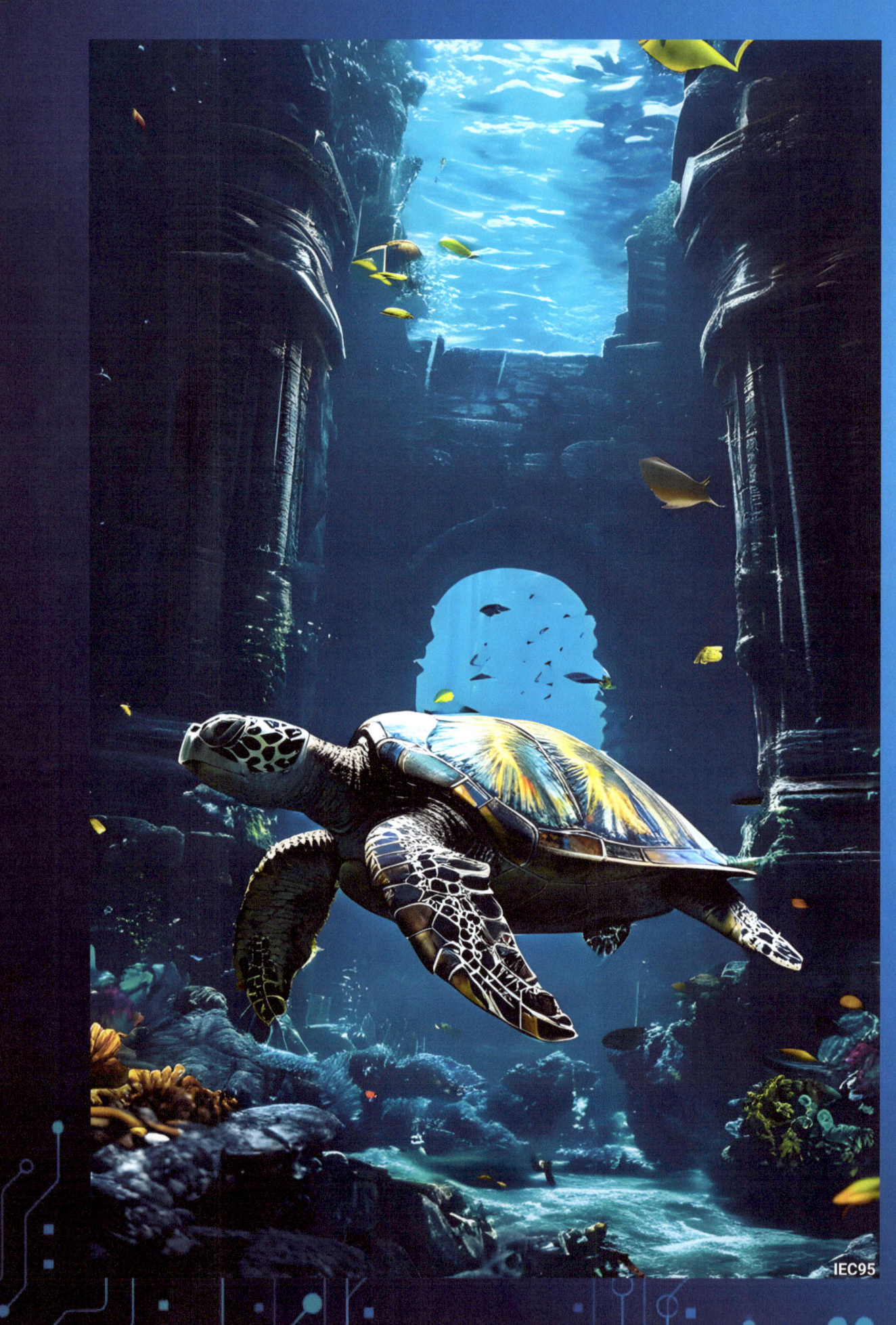
IEC95

6

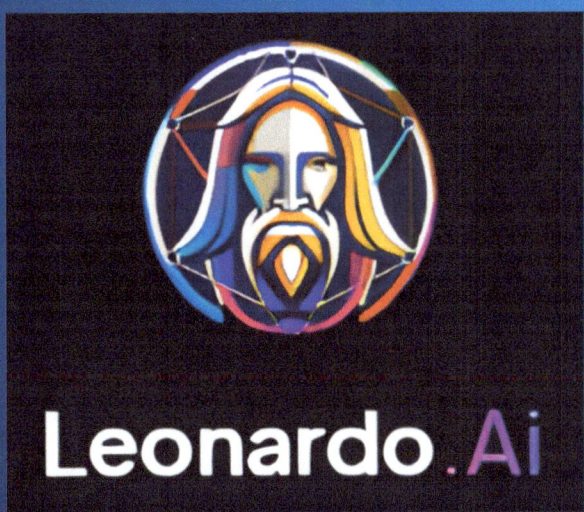

LEONARDO.AI IS AN ARTIFICIAL INTELLIGENCE THAT WORKS WITH A TOKEN PURCHASE SYSTEM TO OBTAIN IMPROVEMENTS AND BENEFITS WHEN CREATING IMAGES BUT IT HAS A FREE VERSION IN WHICH YOU WILL BE GRANTED 150 TOKENS DAILY FOR YOUR CREATIONS.

FIRST YOU HAVE TO CREATE AN ACCOUNT, THEN LAUNCH APP AND FINALLY PRESS THE CREATE NEW IMAGE BUTTON

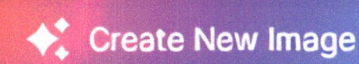

INTERFACE TOOLS

PROMPT

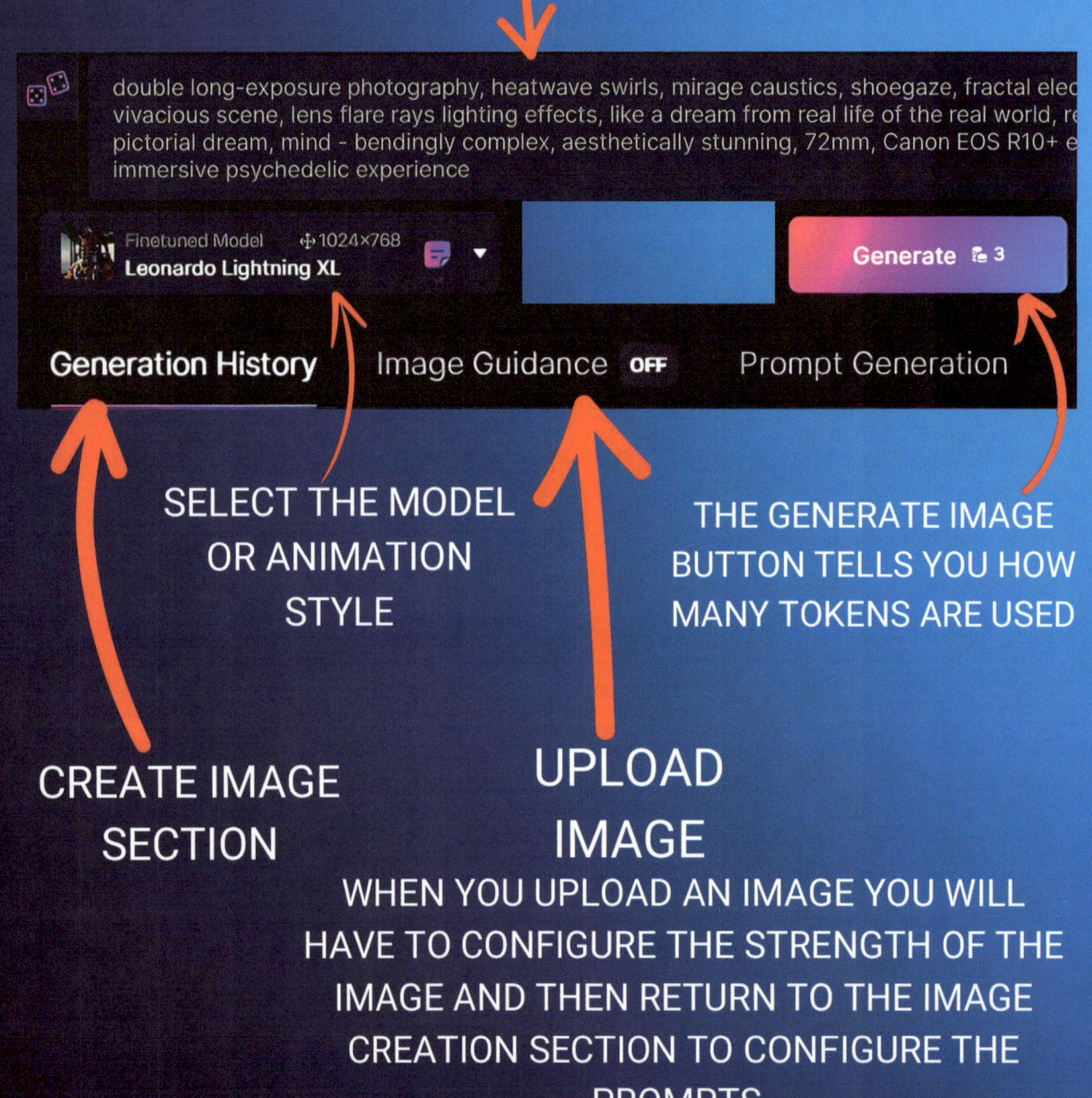

double long-exposure photography, heatwave swirls, mirage caustics, shoegaze, fractal ele
vivacious scene, lens flare rays lighting effects, like a dream from real life of the real world, re
pictorial dream, mind - bendingly complex, aesthetically stunning, 72mm, Canon EOS R10+ e
immersive psychedelic experience

Finetuned Model ⊹ 1024×768
Leonardo Lightning XL

Generate ⬚ 3

Generation History   Image Guidance **OFF**   Prompt Generation

SELECT THE MODEL
OR ANIMATION
STYLE

THE GENERATE IMAGE
BUTTON TELLS YOU HOW
MANY TOKENS ARE USED

UPLOAD
IMAGE

CREATE IMAGE
SECTION

WHEN YOU UPLOAD AN IMAGE YOU WILL
HAVE TO CONFIGURE THE STRENGTH OF THE
IMAGE AND THEN RETURN TO THE IMAGE
CREATION SECTION TO CONFIGURE THE
PROMPTS.

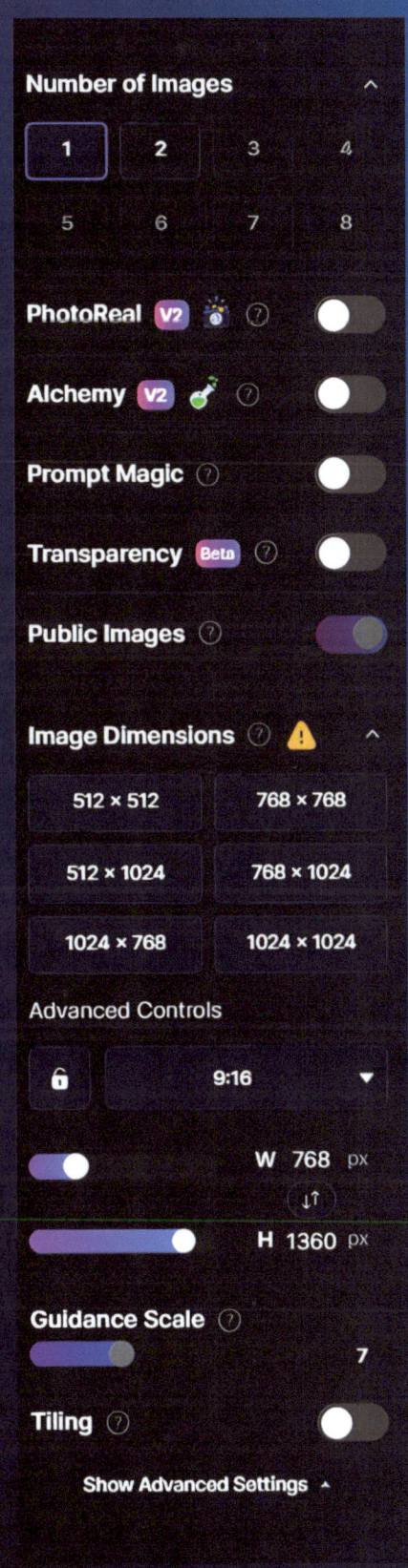

SELECT THE NUMBER OF IMAGES TO BE CREATED

BY PAYING A SUBSCRIPTION YOU CAN USE THESE BENEFITS TO IMPROVE THE QUALITY OF THE IMAGES

MODIFY THE IMAGE DIMENSIONS

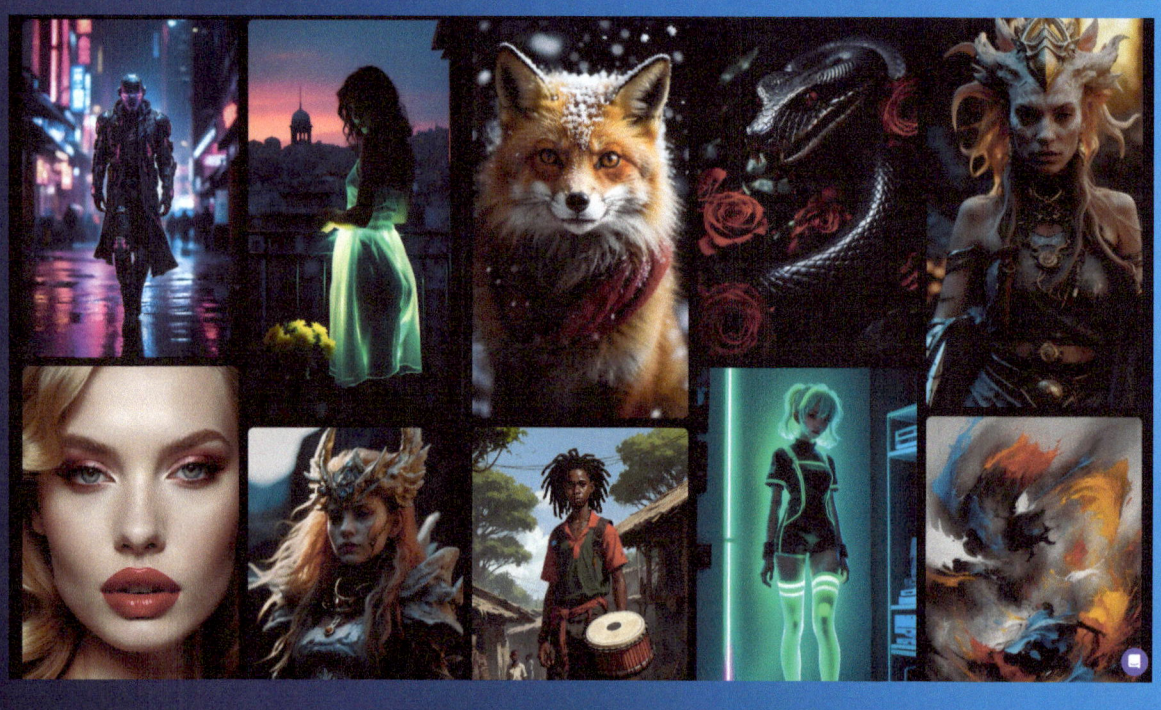

THE LEONARDO.AI COMMUNITY IS ONE OF THE MOST ACTIVE, SO WHEN YOU ENTER THE PLATFORM YOU WILL BE ABLE TO SEE COUNTLESS WORKS DONE BY ITS COMMUNITY.

BY CLICKING ON ONE OF THE COMMUNITY
IMAGES YOU WILL BE ABLE TO SEE THE
DETAILS AND SPECIFICATIONS OF THE IMAGE
AND YOU WILL BE ABLE TO REPLICATE THEM
BY PRESSING THE REMIX BUTTON

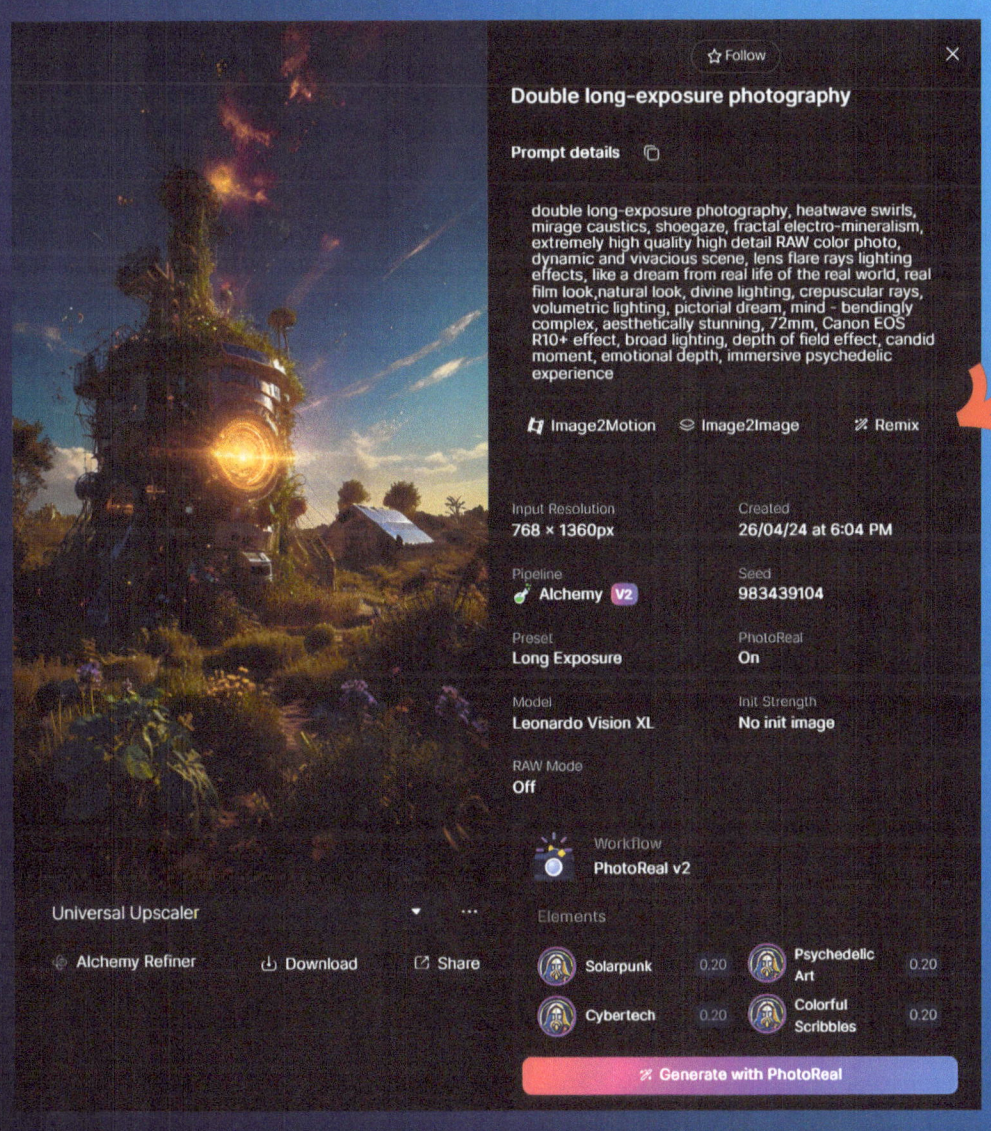

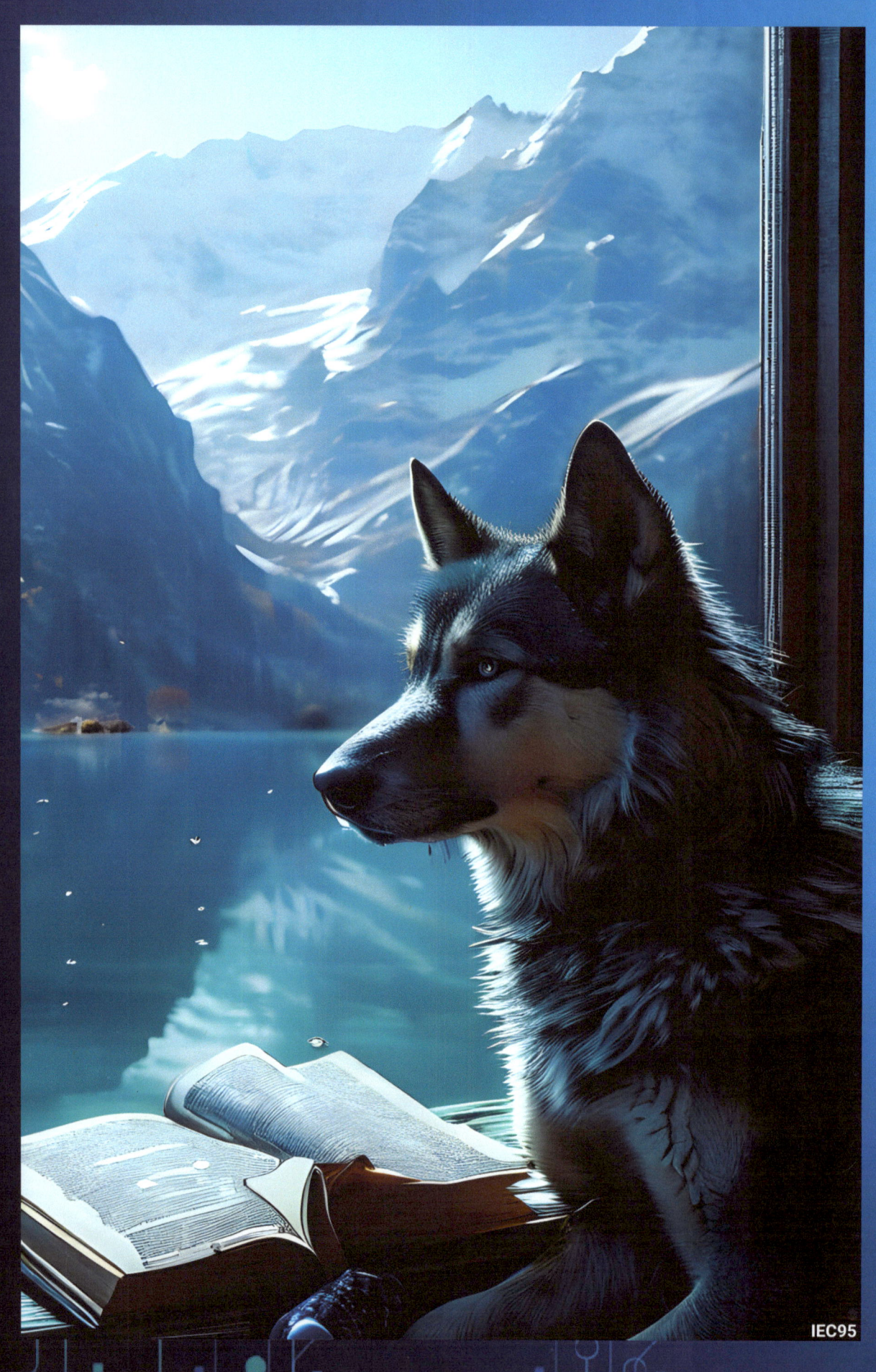

IEC95

"IN THE DIGITAL AGE WE LIVE IN, LEARNING IS MORE ACCESSIBLE THAN EVER. THIS BOOK HAS BEEN CREATED WITH THE GOAL OF PROVIDING AN ACCESSIBLE AND SIMPLE INTRODUCTION TO CREATING IMAGES USING ARTIFICIAL INTELLIGENCE. MY GOAL IN SHARING THIS KNOWLEDGE IS TO HELP PEOPLE OF ALL AGES TO DISCOVER NEW SKILLS AND EXPLORE THE FASCINATING WORLD OF ARTIFICIAL INTELLIGENCE. REMEMBER THAT IT IS NEVER TOO LATE TO LEARN AND THAT KNOWLEDGE IS A POWERFUL TOOL THAT CAN TRANSFORM OUR LIVES. KEEP EXPLORING, KEEP LEARNING, AND NEVER. STOP BEING SURPRISED!"

IF THIS BOOK WAS OF GREAT HELP, I WOULD APPRECIATE A POSITIVE REVIEW FROM YOU, THAT WOULD HELP ME A LOT TO CONTINUE GROWING, GAIN EXPERIENCE AND CREATE BETTER QUALITY CONTENT.

THANK YOU!